WILL I BE BALD IN HEAVEN?

& OTHER CURIOUS QUESTIONS

Published in 2026 by Philo Trust
www.jjohn.com

ISBN (Paperback): 978-1-912326-52-5
ISBN (Digital): 978-1-912326-51-8

Cover Illustration: Dan Kitchener 'DANK' www.dankitchener.com

Print Management by Verité CM Ltd
www.veritecm.com

Printed in the UK

WILL I BE BALD IN HEAVEN?

& OTHER CURIOUS QUESTIONS

J.JOHN

CONTENTS

INTRODUCTION

In its predecessor *Will I Be Fat in Heaven?* I began – perhaps naively – by suggesting that to ask serious and sincere questions was no bad thing. Perhaps because of that I've been inundated by people who, having come up with questions, have asked that I should provide the answers.

That, and the fact that the book pleased a lot of people, has prompted this further set of questions and answers. So here are some forty questions, thirty-nine of which have been raised either by my readers or my friends. These are very varied questions. After all, one aspect of the Christian faith is that it has enormous implications in every area of life. In essence, this book is very similar to the previous book, although I've sought to try to answer very different questions. This is not something to read through from beginning to end in one go. That's a sure recommendation for mental or spiritual indigestion. I'd suggest reading it through question by question.

Since writing the previous book my attention has been drawn to the growing number of those who are respectful of Christianity, admire the culture that the faith has produced, appreciate its worship services, but who are not prepared to make that final, vital step of trust and commitment to Christ as Saviour and Lord. Frankly, they are spectators to the faith when they need to be players. In this context, let me say that what I am defending here is the traditional supernatural faith held by the Christian church from the very earliest days. I believe in a full and deep faith that demands a full and deep commitment.

Three comments about what I've written.

First, these are *personal* answers. So I have selected questions that appeal to me and that I think are important to discuss. I've tried to avoid the sort of detailed Bible riddle such as 'Why, in the Bible text, is the slayer of Goliath given as Elhanan son of Jair in **2 Samuel 21:19** when, as we all know, it was David (**1 Samuel 17**)?' It's a good question but if you want an answer to this sort of thing, I recommend a good study Bible or a commentary. (Answer by the way: it looks like our Hebrew texts of **2 Samuel 21** are missing the phrase 'the brother of' Goliath which is found in **1 Chronicles 20:5**[1]).

Another personal element here is that these are *my* responses to these questions. Although I have sought to stay within what you might label 'mainstream evangelical Christianity faith', these are what have seemed to me to be appropriate responses. Yes, I've consulted with friends and colleagues and dug down into the recesses of my memory for things I've read or heard in the past, but these are my own answers.

[1] https://academic.tyndalehouse.com/explore/articles/who-killed-goliath/. Many modern Bible translations simply insert 'the brother of' into 2 Samuel 21:19.

Second, these are *provisional* answers. Notoriously, we live in a 'post-truth' age and there are those who seem to imagine the truth as something infinitely flexible and perpetually vague. I disagree. I trust the Bible as God's reliable statement of truth. Nevertheless, with some of these questions, any response has to be made from a limited number of biblical statements that were written a long time ago in very different circumstances. Now it's in the nature of things that the questions that are asked in this book are mainly on subjects that are neither specifically dealt with nor treated in depth in the Bible. (No one needs an answer to the question 'Is theft wrong?') The result is that as the Bible has nothing directly to say about such subjects as advertising, social media or even retirement, we are forced to construct and deduce answers based on biblical principles. So inevitably there is a certain caution in some of these responses and I've tried to express that. I've also tried to be very careful about what we can actually say in the absence of data. When God has stayed silent, who am I to speak? And, as ever, it's better to admit you don't know the right answer than to proclaim the wrong one.

Finally, these are *practical* answers. I've no doubt that some of these questions were simply conjured up as a way of offering me a brain-stretching challenge but in others I detect real concern, confusion and sorrow. Some of these questions have been soaked with tears. I have tried to bear this in mind. Furthermore, I take the view that biblical truth is not simply a matter for the head but also for the heart and the will. It is my hope that with some of these answers, after a thoughtful read and an honest prayer, attitudes and actions will be changed.

Finally, what about the fortieth question? Here I've turned things on their head and asked, 'Is it just Christians who face tricky questions?' That has allowed me to write a somewhat longer response suggesting nearly twenty questions that those sceptical of the Christian faith may want to ask themselves. To ask questions is to invite questions in return. It's only fair!

May God bless you through this book and may you come to have a deeper knowledge of the God – Father, Son and Spirit – who is the answer to all questions.

PART ONE

QUESTIONS ABOUT THE BIBLE

1

IS THERE ANY STRUCTURE TO THE BIBLE?

In countless detective films there's a dramatic moment where the hero peers at some text of seemingly random letters and then, with sudden excitement, proclaims, 'Wait! There's a meaning here!' So it is with the Bible. If you were to ask most experts about the structure of the Bible, you would most likely get an answer about it being a compilation of different short books that are collected into the Old and New Testaments. It's a correct answer as far as it goes. But can we go deeper? Is there, in this varied collection of history, poetry, letters and more, a single fundamental, overarching message? Humanly speaking, that would seem unlikely.

After all, the Bible is made up of documents written over 1,200 years by forty different authors from many differing cultures in several different languages. There is no one individual author. Yet with the Bible we don't do ‘humanly speaking’, and I believe behind its text lies God himself as author, and that he has given a structure – a grand narrative – to his book and, with it, a message.

Let’s look at the Bible’s story, and it may help to see it in cinematic terms. The book opens in the most expansive, wide-angle, IMAX way with the creation of the cosmos itself. Rapidly, however, the frame tightens progressively to the earth, to nature and then to human beings. We see them in fellowship with God in a garden paradise which, apart from an off-limits tree of life, they have complete freedom to enjoy. There is reality here but it has a soft-focus, impressionistic quality that defies any *where* and *when* questions. Yet paradise doesn’t endure as, tempted by a diabolic ‘serpent’, the first humans rebel against God and fall under a curse. Separated from God, they are expelled from paradise into a world of pain and toil, with a hint of a future redeemer to comfort them.

When, in **Genesis 11**, Abraham appears, the text suddenly comes into focus and we know where and when we are: the Middle East, 2000 BC. Abraham is given a promise by God that his descendants will not simply be blessed, but will be a blessing to the world.

Turbulent centuries, indeed two millennia, pass. Empires rise and fall around Abraham’s descendants and their nation. Yet the Bible stays focused on the promise of ultimate rescue and blessing for God's people. Great themes emerge and persist. God – *Yahweh* – defines himself as 'the compassionate and gracious God, slow to anger, abounding in love and faithfulness' (**Exodus 34:6**). He shows love to his people through covenants and, in return, expects utter loyalty. The principles of right and wrong are given, first for God's people, but also for the world beyond. We read of priests and a sacrificial system, of prophets and God's word, and of kings who – at least in theory – rule on God's behalf. To the greatest of these kings, David, promises are made of a greater, more perfect king: the *Messiah*.

It's a story with drama: God's people get into trouble, are rescued and get into trouble again. Part of the nation, Samaria, is lost, leaving just a loyal remnant behind. Ultimately, God's people learn the lesson that there is just one God and they must be unshakeably loyal to him. The Old Testament ends on a jarring, unfinished note. God's people are enslaved in their own land and the promised Messiah King has not come.

For the Christian, this incomplete story finds fulfilment in the New Testament. The account of Jesus, descended from David, is told not once, but in four gospels, as if to underline that this is the focal point of the Bible. As we read each gospel we see the narrative slow down: we follow months, weeks and then, at the first Easter, days and even hours.

The grand cosmic scope of **Genesis 1:1** now shrinks to focus on one desolate figure on his cross. No event in the Bible (and indeed none in ancient history) is described with such concentrated detail as the trial and the death of Jesus. This, the Bible announces, is the very heart of its story. It is, to use a significant Latin word, the *crux* – the cross – of the narrative.

Then, with the resurrection of Jesus, with Pentecost and the coming of the Spirit, the tightly framed focus of the Bible starts to zoom dramatically, even explosively, outwards. The good news – the *gospel* – of forgiveness and of the creation of a new and global people in Christ spreads progressively and unstoppably out from the Jews, through the Samaritans, the Gentiles and then to Rome, the centre of the known world.

The Bible does not stop there. At the very end of **Revelation (chapters 20 to 22)** we return to the grand widescreen, soft-focus view of the first chapters. But now the tone is gloriously different. The themes announced at the beginning of **Genesis** now return in triumphant fulfilment. In a magnificent account, full of echoes of the past, we see how the serpent, now unmasked as Satan, has been destroyed and the curse, with its sorrow, pain and death, is no more. Christ, the victorious King, reigns among his people who now have fellowship with him in a new garden (and city) in which the tree of life is now freely accessible.

I cannot imagine how this awesome symmetrical structure can be the creation of human beings and in it I see the hand of the great Author, God. He has given us a book that points to the one specific individual, Christ, and the one event, his cross, which can answer the need all humans have for forgiveness and hope. On the cross of Christ stands the redemption of the whole universe and, with it, our own hope of eternal joy. For believers, this is our own story.

2

HOW IS THE OLD TESTAMENT RELEVANT TO US TODAY?

For many people today, the Old Testament has an image problem. It's a daunting length and speaks of an intimidatingly unfamiliar culture, with strange names, long genealogies, peculiar customs, sacrifices and a splattering of bloodshed. (Mind you, such things are no deterrent to successful screen fantasy series.) Even the name *Old* can be off-putting, somehow implying obsolescence, a status that seems confirmed by the New Testament's references to a '*new* covenant' and its shift of focus from the temple, the land and the Law to Jesus, the kingdom of God and the whole world.

Notwithstanding that, I believe the Old Testament is relevant today. Let me give you four reasons.

- Jesus and the writers of the New Testament constantly refer to the Old Testament. They saw it as a book written under God's supervision that provided an authoritative source of truth. That's recommendation enough.

- The Old Testament reveals who God is. In it we see not just his holiness, justice and perfection but also his tender love and faithfulness and his willingness to be committed to his people by covenants.
- The Old Testament explains the setting in which Jesus spoke. From it we learn such things as why the Jewish people kept themselves so separate, were committed to God and were devoted to the religious Law, the Sabbath, a kosher diet and the temple-based system of festivals, priests and sacrifices. In it we find the vital 'backstory' to the New Testament.
- To know the Old Testament guards against some of the outlandish views of Jesus which, for example, treat him as a mystical Eastern guru or some Greek philosopher. No, Jesus was Jewish, as were most of his hearers, and we need to know the Old Testament to see him in that context.

Yet we can go further and deeper. As I pointed out in responding to Question 1, the Bible is the 'great story' and given that three-quarters of it is the Old Testament, it cannot be overlooked.

The Old Testament shows four things relevant to the 'great story'.

First, the Old Testament declares human *failure*. Throughout its many pages we read a harsh but needed evaluation of humanity. Although we men and women are made in God's image and greatly loved by him, we have, from the beginning, defied him to the extent that rebellion has become part of our existence. Put bluntly, we are all sinners. The Old Testament Law, summarised in the Ten Commandments, lays down God's moral standard and, in doing so, demonstrates how far short of it we all fall. The Old Testament does more than merely define sin, it demonstrates sin's power and range by showing how even such towering figures as Moses, David and Elijah, at some point stumbled and fell.

We see too that although God created the offices of prophets, priests and kings to bring stability and guidance to a disordered world, even these do not escape being contaminated by sin. In fact, so ingrained is the human inclination towards wrong that even our attempts to redeem ourselves through religion not merely fail but actually make things worse. Ultimately, the Old Testament states the stark and uncomfortable truth that we human beings cannot redeem ourselves. Only God can.

Second, the Old Testament is a *foretelling*. If the Old Testament bluntly rules out us rescuing ourselves, it holds out the hope that God will. As a start, God offers a measure of forgiveness through the sacrificial system. Yet the Old Testament looks beyond this and tells – in prophecies and promises – of a Messiah, a glorious Saviour who will be a perfect prophet, priest and king. Parallel to this comes the promise of a suffering servant, a supreme figure who will himself be a sacrifice for God's people. It will take the first Easter to reveal how one person could be both Saviour and Servant.

Third, the Old Testament prepares for *fulfilment*.
It provides the setting for Jesus to come as God's rescuer for humanity. Here the Old Testament performs three vital roles. One is how the fulfilment of its prophecies by Jesus confirms that he is indeed the long-promised rescuer. Another is how, in the light of the Old Testament's ruthless cataloguing of human failure, Jesus – the only individual in the whole Bible without fault or failing – is supreme. Still another is how fully Jesus takes up every Old Testament office, becoming the ultimate and perfect prophet, priest and king, and wields authority over human beings, disease, demons and even death.

In fact, in a manner his opponents considered outrageous, Jesus took on the role of the temple, offering direct and personal forgiveness in himself. Jesus was in no doubt that the Old Testament spoke about him, saying on one occasion to his critics, 'You study the Scriptures diligently because you think that in them you have eternal life. These are the very Scriptures that testify about me' (**John 5:39**).

Finally, the Old Testament is a *foundation*. It reveals our need for rescue, promises God's rescue and confirms Jesus as the great Rescuer. But it goes beyond that. Those of us who have been rescued by Jesus can return to the Old Testament that once accused us to find out how we should now live. Although many of the trappings of the Law have been abolished by Christ and his cross, the essentials persist to guide our lives as a thankful response to God's grace. As God's children we are aided in keeping the Law through God's Spirit, and when we fail we can know God's forgiveness in Christ.

Our Old Testament was the Bible of Jesus and the early church. It therefore should be ours too!

3

WHY DO I FIND SO MUCH OF THE BIBLE BORING?

The issue many people have with the Bible, particularly the Old Testament, is not that it seems irrelevant, but that they find it uninteresting, even boring. Here I don't just want to answer the question 'why?' I want to suggest remedies.

One reason for finding the Old Testament boring is false expectations. Some, perhaps fresh from an adrenaline-rich diet of sagas or superheroes, may be disappointed at the lack of thrills. Others, wanting only comforting or consoling words, may suffer an equal disappointment. While there are passages of both excitement and consolation, to insist on them is to misunderstand the God-given purpose of the Old Testament. It is about who God is; how, in love and justice, he has begun to deal with the human problem of sin and what he expects from his people in response. All this is recorded in a compilation of history, prophecy, poetry, preaching and even legal documents and family records.

A second reason is the cultural chasm between our world and that of the Bible, particularly the Old Testament. Most of that book was written originally for people in a harsh agricultural environment, living out their short earthly existence in extended families in male-dominated communities that they rarely left. They were individuals fiercely committed to their relatives, tribe and nation, and of course, to their religion with its priests, sacrifices and laws. Culturally, we are very unlike them.

A third reason lies in how the Old Testament was written. Its writers hadn't the luxury of such tools as footnotes, appendices, different fonts and even text boxes. It's possible that if something like Leviticus was written today, much of it might be in footnotes and appendices. Equally, we fail to appreciate how much of the Old Testament text originated as the spoken word. So its habit of repetition, something we struggle with, would have been an essential part of how it was recited aloud in a community. We are equally unsympathetic about the length of many biblical accounts. Today, in our age of haste we demand brevity but we may be unwise to do so. After all, there is much – from pregnancy to winemaking – that needs time. Not everything can be said in a smartphone text message.

The final reason is that we need to realise that the Old Testament is relevant. Every Christian has a personal involvement in that part of the Bible. It was written for God's ancient people but these men and women are, in a sense deeper than genetics, our ancestors. Spiritually, their story is our family history.

Let me suggest remedies against boredom under the following headings. However, I must say that if you find *all* the Bible boring *all* the time, then you may want to examine your relationship with God. Many Christians can recount how they found the Bible impenetrably dull until they came to a personal faith in Jesus.

- ***Translation.*** To read ancient accounts in ancient translations multiplies problems. Modern translations, such as the NIV (New International Version) or the NLT (New Living Translation), are much easier to read than older ones.

- ***Information.*** A study Bible, with the text and helpful background material, can be a help. Of the many available, I prefer those which seek to simply explain the Bible rather than impose any theological or denominational agenda. Beware the danger, though, of paying more attention to the human notes than to the divine text. I use two Bibles: one to read for spiritual nourishment and a study Bible to consult for reference. At a deeper level lies the whole world of commentaries on individual Bible books.

- ***Expectation.*** Quite simply, we need to expect God to speak through his word. Remember its relevance and keep asking one simple question: *so what?* How is what I'm reading relevant for my life? Is there a rebuke? A challenge? An encouragement? *If you want to hear God speak, read the Bible.* If you want to hear God speak audibly, read it out loud! The Bible is the only book that everyone in the world can read along with the author.

- ***Determination.*** Getting the most out of the Old Testament takes effort. Here there are several aids. One is a good Bible study group. Many people have found that difficult passages can come alive amongst others. Equally, the good Bible study groups teach good habits. There are also helpful books. Gordon Fee and Douglas Stewart have produced two excellent ones: *How to Read the Bible for All its Worth and How to Read the Bible Book by Book.*

- ***Contemplation.*** Although the Bible is food for the soul, it is not *fast* food. Take time to study a passage, read it, re-read it and meditate on it. Above all, pray! All Scripture is inspired by God's Holy Spirit and given that he lives in all who have trusted in Christ, it's sound sense to ask him to open a passage and give us something to feed on from it.

- ***Proportion.*** Have a sense of balance. Although the New Testament says that 'All Scripture is God-breathed and is useful for teaching, rebuking, correcting and training in righteousness' (2 Timothy 3:16), I don't think it means that all Scripture is *equally* useful for teaching, etc. In fact a sensible approach to personal Bible reading is that of a 'mixed menu'. You can do this by following a Bible reading plan and I recommend that of Robert Murray M'Cheyne which my wife Killy and I followed for many years. An informal alternative is simply to make three bookmarks: put one at the beginning of Genesis, one at the beginning of the Psalms and one at the beginning of the New Testament. Proceeding from each of these, read three chapters (or more) of the Bible each day.

Above all, persist in reading the Bible. It's a universal experience of Christians that the more you read the Bible, the more you understand it. Just do it!

4

HAS THE BIBLE BEEN CHANGED?

There are various reasons for people talking about the Bible being 'changed'. In the secular West today one reason seems to be either to erase Jesus from history entirely or to replace the towering, authoritative figure of the gospels with a watered-down 'Jesus', a shadowy being who affirms everybody and condemns no one. Still others, from their own religious viewpoint, consider the Bible to be 'corrupted' because it contradicts their own sacred book.

Let me first clarify what the Bible is. The Bible is not a book of rules, but rather an account and a proclamation of how God offers forgiveness to all humanity in Jesus. In Christianity, we do not do what is right in order to be forgiven by God, but as a grateful response for having been forgiven by him. The result is the Bible is not so much *instruction* as *invitation*.

This view of the Bible helps us understand what change means. For one thing, the Bible has always been translated –

after all there's not much point in sending out an invitation if no one understands it! And, by definition, to make a translation is to change a text. In fact, Bible translations are constantly revised as better understandings of the ancient manuscripts emerge and as modern languages change. One helpful idea here is to consider the Bible not as some fixed and framed statement of rules, with every letter inscribed unchangeably for eternity, but instead more like a glass window that allows us to look through, to see Jesus and to have eternal life. As such, the task of those who translate the Bible is to make and keep the window as clean as possible to allow the book's central figure to be seen clearly.

Behind many of these claims of 'change' lies the idea that the Bible, or more specifically the New Testament that we have, does not authentically represent God's message to humanity. For a fuller response than I can give here I would refer you to any decent account of the transmission of Bible texts. I cover part of this in *Jesus Christ – The Truth* with Chris Walley, but to go deeper I'd suggest the full-length study by Peter Williams entitled *Can We Trust the Gospels?* published by Crossway.

In antiquity the New Testament was always a treasured book and, as such, was carefully preserved and copied. The result is that a massive number (25,000) of fragmentary, partial or complete copies of the New Testament in Greek and other languages exist, some dating back to the second century. As the entire New Testament is preserved in the *Codex Sinaiticus* and *Codex Vaticanus* of around AD 350, any sort of substantial change to the biblical text after this time can be eliminated.

Some idea of how limited the changes to the Bible are can be seen by comparing the King James or Authorised Version of 1611 with a modern English version. The language has been updated to reflect modern English usage and there are a few other slight changes. So, based on the vastly more numerous texts available today, a handful of passages in the old version are now relegated to footnotes; notably **Mark 16:9-20**, **John 7:53 – 8:11** and **1 John 5:7-8**. Significantly, the first two passages were already considered questionable by Erasmus as early as 1516. But none of the changes make any difference to the Bible's message.

Let me note that those who claim the Bible has been substantially changed, cannot explain how, when, why and by whom any changes were made. The commonest suggestion is that a Jesus of Nazareth existed but was no more than some travelling teacher who offered wise words and who, after his death on the cross, was mysteriously elevated to the rank of Messiah and God.

In reality, there are many diverse lines of evidence that confirm the biblical picture of Jesus as an historic individual associated with both extraordinary claims and extraordinary actions and who, after his public death (in April, AD 33), returned to life.

Here are a few.

- Historians tell us the Christian community in Rome was sufficiently large to be made a scapegoat by Nero for the fire of AD 64. We know too for a fact that by the end of the first century, the Christian population of what is now Turkey was large enough that the authorities considered believers a social threat. Such explosive growth of the faith is very odd indeed if Jesus was no more than a purely human teacher in one of the empire's remoter corners.

- If the gospels were the creation of the early church, presumably based in the Greek-speaking northern Mediterranean margin, then it's very strange that they so accurately reflect the distinctive and very different religious, cultural and geographic settings in which they describe Jesus.

- There are striking omissions in the gospels that speak of authenticity. The early Christian church debated many things, such as circumcision, diet, relations with Gentiles and church management. It would have been very convenient to have some ruling from Jesus on such matters. But there are no such rulings.

- There are a half-dozen or so letters that even sceptics agree were written by the apostle Paul before the mid-60s AD and so within thirty years of the first Easter. In all of them Jesus is referred to as a cosmic being who in some way is God. **1 Corinthians**, universally dated as AD 53 to 55, has a whole chapter centred around the certainty that Jesus rose bodily from the dead.

Has the Bible been changed? No, not in any substantial way. It does what it always did – showing us how to come to God through Jesus Christ. There is no reason to doubt its great comfort to those who believe it. Nor its hard challenge to those who don't.

5

WAS THE UNIVERSE CREATED IN A LITERAL SIX DAYS?

In recent years, the 'creation debate' within Christianity has warmed up and not in a good way; there's a lot more heat than light around. In many church circles there is now a Young Earth Creation (YEC) view holding to a universe only 6,000 years old and a global flood depositing all rocks and creating every aspect of the earth's surface around 2300 BC. As a reminder, this is several million times younger than that of the current scientific consensus of a universe forming around 13.8 billion years ago and the earth 4.54 billion years ago.

Let me make three initial comments.

- Although the term *creationist* is often carelessly used only for those holding a YEC view, all Christians are creationists because we believe that the universe was created by God.

- The age of the earth is a separate issue to that of evolution, which I will address in Question 23. Whether a Christian can believe in evolution depends on how you define it.

- The idea of a bitter conflict between faith and science is talked up, by not just some Christians but also atheists. Sceptics enjoy Christians insisting on such things as a variable speed of light, all rocks deposited by the flood and dinosaurs on the ark.

The ultimate issue with **Genesis 1** is that of interpretation. We need to distinguish between a *literal* interpretation where we read the passage in the sense *that the author intended it to be read*, and a *literalistic* interpretation where, ignoring context or figures of speech, we treat the words at face value. A literalistic interpretation of someone's claim to be 'heartbroken' would have us send them to a cardiologist quickly.

Over the ages, many people – but not all – took **Genesis 1** to literally be history. Yet beginning over 200 years ago (before any theory of evolution), there was a dawning recognition that the universe looked very much older. Science identified evidence of a long history of the earth, with mountains built up and worn down, the perpetual recycling of rocks and such things as granite masses that demanded many thousands of years to solidify from liquid. Parallel to this, astronomers began describing a universe that was enormous in scale and which, given the fixed speed of light, was necessarily old. A more recent testimony to a very old earth is that we can see, through plate tectonics, how continents repeatedly divide, slide and collide with each other in a process demanding either millions of years or a multitude of miracles.

But does Genesis 1 demand we understand it in a literalistic way? Many people have pointed out that the meaning of the Hebrew word for 'day' is very broad. So, for example, in the Hebrew of **Genesis 2:4** the entire sequence of creation is referred to as occurring 'in the *day* that the Lord God made the earth and the heavens'. And then there's an interesting question as to whose days these are: mortal humans or a timeless God? There are other questions. How long is a day before the sun was created? How does light appear on the first day and plants on the third but the sun – essential for both – only on the fourth day? How does Adam manage to name all the animals in a single sixth day? What does history mean before there were human beings?

Many Bible scholars have highlighted the curious structure of **Genesis 1**, with the first three days describing the forming of things and the last three days their filling. So Day 1 is about light and dark, Day 2 about sea and sky, and Day 3 land and vegetation. Paralleling these are Day 4 with the lights that rule day and night, Day 5 with the rulers of sea and sky, and

Day 6 with the animals and humankind to rule the land. On Day 7 – God rested. One possibility – and no more – is that what we have is not so much a historical document as a topical and legal one, laying out realms and their rulers. Given the widespread use of legal, covenant language throughout the Bible, such a view has merit.

Part of our problem is that, in an age governed by science, we are tempted to read **Genesis 1** as if it was a scientific text. Yet this part of the Genesis account may perhaps be 4,000 years old and was given for all people of all times of all cultures, whether scientific or not. It addresses the truly important questions of the *who* and the *why* of creation rather than the much less important ones of the *when* and the *how*. Let's let Genesis be Genesis!

Frankly, I'm not sure how Genesis and science match but I am certain of three things. The first is that I'd rather have an open question than a wrong answer. Second, as Francis Schaeffer said, here there must be 'no final conflict'. Finally, as an evangelist, let me insist that the issue of the age of the earth must not obscure or distract from the matter that lies at the very heart of the Bible: Jesus Christ, the Way, the Truth and the Life.

6

HOW ARE WE SUPPOSED TO UNDERSTAND THOSE LONG LIFESPANS IN GENESIS?

In reading Genesis chapters 5 and 11, we encounter people with very long lifespans: Adam living to 930 years (**Genesis 5:5**), Methuselah to 969 (**Genesis 5:27**) and Noah to 950 (**Genesis 9:29**). This extraordinary longevity continues after the flood although the ages are lower and soon decline, with Abraham living to 175 (**Genesis 25:7**) and Moses to 120 (**Deuteronomy 34:7**). A related feature is the high age, averaging 156, at which these men fathered their first child. These lifespans are significant because they have been used to construct a timetable for ancient biblical history, giving a date for Adam around 4000 BC and the flood at 2300 BC.

There are, however, two problems with these long lifespans. The most obvious is that they do not fit with human experience. In **Psalm 90**, attributed to Moses, we read, 'Our days may come to seventy years, or eighty, if our strength endures' (**Psalm 90:10**). Thousands of years later, that figure has barely changed, with the average lifespan in the developed world now around seventy-five for men and eighty for women. They don't fit with history either: studies of skeletons reveal that, unsurprisingly, life expectancy was lower in the past and in the Bronze Age, where these Genesis dates belong, it was probably around forty. In fact, there seems to be a biological limit to human life, with very few people living beyond a hundred and the longest verified life being 122.

Now I have no problems with taking these Genesis texts at face value and God miraculously giving people long lives. Yet there are other issues here.

One is that these ages seem inconsistent with themselves and the biblical narrative. So, taken as facts, they give overlapping lives. Noah's 950-year-long life means he would have been Abraham's contemporary for fifty-eight years, with his son Shem outliving Abraham by thirty-five years. But there are no hints of this, or other similar overlapping lives. Now consider Abraham himself. In **Genesis 17:17** he expresses incredulity that a hundred-year-old man and a ninety-year-old woman might produce children. Yet why is he so surprised? His immediate ancestors – one of whom is seemingly still alive – had children when they were several hundred years old. Note, too, how in **Genesis 15:15**

God promises Abraham that he will be buried at a good old age, something echoed in **Genesis 25:8** where we read that he 'died at a good old age, an old man and full of years'. Yet by the standards of his multi-centennial ancestors, Abraham's 175 years was not a 'good old age' at all; it was a life cut tragically short.

Here we must remember these are ancient documents. Elements of **Genesis 1 to 11** have parallels – although far more amazing on Mesopotamian clay tablets dated somewhere between 2900 and 2000 BC. These are of interest because Abraham – the father of God's people – originated in Mesopotamia. If the Genesis texts are of a similar age or even older, they come out of a culture with which we are very unfamiliar. It is this antiquity that gives many people the sense that here we are seeing history in 'focus'.

Let me outline some proposed explanations of these long ages.

One explanation is that these are not the lifetimes of a single individual but of a lineage or several generations. So Methuselah's age might in reality be for 'Methuselah, his sons, grandsons,' etc. Although it's a possible solution – after all, the genealogy of Jesus in **Matthew 1** jumps generations – the fact is that Enoch and Noah are both clearly treated as individuals.

Another explanation is that these numbers are symbolic, something that the first readers or hearers would have recognised. Some point out the ancient Jewish tradition of *gematria* in which names are turned into numbers. Yet, if this is the case, it's a code we haven't cracked.

One intriguing explanation draws on these Mesopotamian tablets, which bear what is called the Sumerian King List, a semi-mythological account of history. The kings here have astonishingly extended lifespans. One striking parallel with Genesis is that these accounts record a flood event with shorter life spans occurring afterwards. Possibly related is the fact that the Mesopotamian mathematical system was very different from that used by the Hebrews. So there have been suggestions that, in the same way a figure measured in metres might be misread if understood as being in feet, there was a misunderstanding in the long process of the transmission of these records.

Whatever their origin, these long ages have a significant theological role. In the Bible, Adam and Eve are portrayed as having had the potential for eternal life but, by rejecting it through their rebellion against God, allowed death to enter human existence. These progressively falling lifespans in Genesis act as a reminder of how sin and decay progressively crept into human existence.

So, while future research on the ancient world may cast some light on this, at the moment there are no illuminating answers. In the meantime, let me point out that most of us are unimpressed with the idea of living for hundreds of years. We do not want length of life, we want quality. It is precisely this better, richer life that is promised us through Christ. As **Romans 6:23** says, 'For the wages of sin is death, but the gift of God is eternal life in Christ Jesus our Lord.' *Amen!*

7

DOES THE BIBLE CONDONE SLAVERY?

Some critics of Christianity claim that the church has condoned slavery and even that the Bible itself is pro-slavery. Let's examine the issue.

Although definitions are tricky, to be a slave is to be treated as no more than a possession, to lose the right of freedom, to work without pay and to be utterly humiliated. In considering slavery, we must remember that what comes to mind, the brutal, racial enslavement of black people in the USA that endured until 1865, is not the only form of slavery. Other forms of slavery have existed. We need to note too the unhappy truth that slavery has been practised by almost every culture and race. Some of the oldest written records, from around 3500 BC, reveal it was a fact of life in Mesopotamia. Sadly, too, slavery is no extinct practice. Although technically illegal everywhere, there are some estimates that worldwide, 50 million men, women and children still exist in slavery. We must recognise too that slavery is essentially hinted at in many unjust employment practices, some of which are slavery in all but name.

Slavery appears in both the Old and New Testaments, and to understand how to deal with it we need to think about the Bible. Many people imagine the Bible to be a single, final message that God downloaded from heaven at one particular moment in time. In fact, the Christian belief is that God gave his word to humanity over at least two thousand years through human authors writing in their own time and culture in what has been called 'progressive revelation'. This is like a plant which starts with a shoot and then, over time, produces a stalk and then a bud until, finally, a flower blooms. So Christians would see the full and final blossoming of God's message to humanity occurring in Jesus (**Hebrews 1:1-2**). This doesn't mean the entire Old Testament can be thrown away – Jesus and the apostles quoted from it – it's simply that, for Christians, parts need to be treated in the light of the New Testament.

Certainly slavery was accepted in the early part of the Old Testament but the rules under which it was allowed were strict and an advance on practices in neighbouring nations. While Israelites could only be taken as slaves if they chose this as a means of paying off debts, the enslavement of foreigners was accepted. Nevertheless, they were considered fellow human beings and had privileges and protections. Encouragement for the kind treatment of slaves came from the memory that the Israelites had themselves been slaves under the Egyptians. By the time of the later Old Testament, slavery as an institution seems to have died out amongst Jews. This tolerance of a moderated slavery in a part of the Old Testament does not greatly perturb Christians today: we see the relevant passages as no longer being applicable.

In the New Testament world slavery was widely practised amongst Romans and Greeks. One result is the use in the New Testament of the Greek word *doulos*. Although sometimes translated as 'slave' or 'servant' it refers to a 'bond-servant'; someone who belonged to another person and, while not free, could be educated, accumulate wealth, own property and even have slaves of their own. Jesus himself makes no direct ruling on slavery, although a number of his parables mention slavery and he uses the imagery of a 'bond-servant' for himself and his followers. Nevertheless, in his great summary of the Law, Jesus says, 'Love your neighbour as yourself' (Matthew 22:39) and by doing so, utterly cuts the ground from underneath the whole system of slavery.

The letters of the New Testament adopt a similar, ultimately subversive, strategy. In Ephesians 6:5, Colossians 3:22

and **1 Peter 2:18**, slaves are encouraged to be obedient and loyal, yet although the letters use the language of slavery, they do not approve it. In fact, by proclaiming that Christian slaves and their masters are brothers and sisters, the whole practice of slavery is made utterly indefensible. Equally, racially based slavery is rendered invalid by the declaration that God has overcome all racial divisions at the cross (**Ephesians 2:11-22; Galatians 3:28**).

In this double strategy of not challenging slavery openly but quietly undermining it I see a pragmatic wisdom. Slavery was fundamental to the Roman economy – a third of Rome's population were slaves – and revolts were savagely repressed. Any attempt by Christians to directly confront slavery would have been disastrous.

Given the teaching of the New Testament, I wish I could say that when Christianity became the moral authority in Europe, the practice of slavery ended. The reality, sadly, is much more mixed.[2] Nevertheless, by AD 1000 slavery had largely ended in the Christian parts of Europe. Sadly, it returned – and on an 'industrial scale' – in the plantations of the New World. The final abolition of slavery in the West was, as universally admitted, largely driven by Evangelicals and Quakers, with the continuing practice of the enslavement of Africans by other Africans strongly opposed by missionaries.

[2] For a detailed and balanced study of the church's achievements and failures in the area of slavery, historian Tom Holland's 600-page book *Dominion, the Making of the Western Mind* is invaluable.

So while the Bible may display a toleration of the slavery of its day, it ultimately makes the practice morally impossible. Less easy to defend is how, for centuries, Christians failed to recognise this. Nevertheless, although Christianity's record is flawed, it is important to note that the most sustained opposition against slavery has come from within the Christian faith.

Yes, the slavery of the past was utterly appalling. But there are many parts of the world today where people are working in conditions that are in fact little more than slavery. In condemning past injustices, let's not ignore modern ones.

PART TWO

QUESTIONS ABOUT GOD

8

IF GOD CREATED THE UNIVERSE, WHO CREATED GOD?

The question as to who – or what – created God is, I think, one that everybody has asked. After all, in our experience, everything has to come from something but where does any ultimate original *something* come from?

If you pick up any book of theology, you will find this aspect of God is treated. God, we are told, is eternal: he always was, always is and always will be. He is a timeless being with no beginning and no end. Well, I'm not going to argue with that. Let's see if we can go a bit further.

On a matter like this, as with everything else to do with God, the only data we can absolutely rely on is what God has said about himself in the Bible. Perhaps the key passage is where God reveals himself to Moses in the burning bush in **Exodus 3**. This is a vital text because it is here that God reveals his identity and his purposes to Moses and, through him, to the Israelites. Names were important in this culture and Moses asks God who he is and what his name is. God responds, 'I AM WHO I AM. This is what you are to say to the Israelites: "I AM has sent me to you"' (**Exodus 3:14**). In the next verse God gives his name as Yahweh (normally translated as the LORD in English), a name that is linked with 'I AM'. Now, mountains of books have been written on this but the general conclusion is that God is declaring he is eternal, utterly independent and totally unchanging. Years, centuries, millennia pass, but God does not alter.

Other Bible verses pick up this theme. So in **Isaiah 57:15** we read, 'For this is what the high and exalted One says – he who lives forever, whose name is holy.' **Psalm 90:2**: 'Before the mountains were born or you brought forth the whole world, from everlasting to everlasting you are God.' The New Testament also points out the eternity of God: '"I am the Alpha and the Omega," says the Lord God, "who is, and who was, and who is to come, the Almighty"' (**Revelation 1:8**). There is a similar sense of God's timelessness in **2 Peter 3:8**: 'With the Lord a day is like a thousand years, and a thousand years are like a day.'

One fascinating, if incidental, insight into the relationship of God and time is seen in Jesus' response when he was challenged over his claim to be superior to Abraham: 'Before Abraham was born, I am!' (**John 8:58**). Here, in an extraordinary way, Jesus is not only taking God's title 'I AM' for himself but he is also saying something profound about his existence. He doesn't merely say, 'Before Abraham was born, *I was*', which would have been remarkable, but rather '*I am*'. This implies that Jesus is eternal.

But what does the idea that God is eternal actually mean? Obviously this is something that we cannot begin to comprehend properly and here a reverent humility is in order. However, one idea that some people find helpful is to imagine an artist creating a series of pictures that portray events, perhaps even some sort of graphic novel. Within the pictures, and for their inhabitants, there is a succession of actions but the artist, beyond the images, stands outside that created time and so is able to see it all. The idea that God can see beyond all time, of course, explains how he can be certain of the future and make prophecies about it.

Ultimately, in asking, 'Who created God?' we are asking an unanswerable question. Perhaps the simplest response is to suggest that we are like a cartoon character asking who drew the artist!

Let me end this question with two points. The first is that anyone who's ever engaged in talking about origins will have faced the question, 'Well then, who made God?' often delivered with an air of aggressive confidence as if it was the ultimate weapon that utterly destroyed all Christian arguments.

Of course it isn't that simple. All discussions about what you might call 'ultimate origins' end up with problems that cannot be solved. Take the currently accepted view that time, space and the universe originated from the Big Bang, the sudden expansion – the flowering – of some original superhot and super dense 'singularity'. But here, of course, a similar question arises. Where did this singularity come from? Frankly, if it's a choice between an eternal God making everything and a nothing giving rise to everything, I know where my vote goes.

My final point is this. Can I suggest that there is both blessing and risk in focusing on a God who is so utterly beyond our comprehension? The blessing lies in the way that we are reminded of the greatness of God. As the helpful saying goes, 'Little God, big problems; big God, little problems.' Yet the risk is that we fix our thinking on a God so utterly beyond our comprehension and so inaccessible that we find any relationship with him difficult. The awesome, dazzling truth at the heart of Christianity is that, in Jesus, this breathtakingly glorious God has actually come down to be with us. So in all his awesomeness, we can know him as 'Father'.

9

WHY ISN'T GOD MORE OBVIOUS?

As an evangelist, I regularly get asked questions such as 'I'm searching for God. Why isn't he more obvious?' I'm tempted to ask what sort of evidence they want. A constellation in the night sky that spells out 'Repent and believe'? A segment found in every strand of DNA that says 'Made by God!' or some fundamental constant in the universe that, when decoded to the millionth decimal place, reads '**John 3:16**'? Instead, let me make a deeper, and I hope more helpful, response by what may seem a circuitous route.

Our human experience is traditionally considered in terms of our 'head, heart and will'. The 'head' refers to our intellect, thinking and our reason. So, for example, someone may say, 'I've been using my head to analyse the situation.' The 'heart', of course, is the emotions and so someone may admit, 'Oh, I knew the house was a ruin when I bought it, but I was led by my heart.' The 'will' represents determination, decision and drive as when someone says, 'I recognised it was going to be a difficult job but I was determined to do it.'

Ideally, we want these three aspects of our experience to work together but that doesn't always happen. In fact the conflict between head, heart and will is the stuff of enormous drama in both fiction and reality. It can be particularly problematic in the matter of finding a life partner. 'Falling in love' is, of course, an affair of the heart, but nevertheless head and will play their part. Yet imagine how someone might feel if, over some cosy meal together, the individual sitting opposite says, 'Look, I don't have any strong emotional feelings towards you, but my head tells me you'd be the right person to marry. Will you?' I think the answer might well be 'no' on the not unreasonable basis that at least some 'heart' element is essential for any sort of profound lasting relationship. (Let me add that there have been many marriages that began on a rather cool basis and many have been successful. But that's another story.)

Significantly, how we respond to human beings also applies to how we respond to God. After all, we are made in his image and he too is a person. When Jesus was asked what the greatest commandment was, he replied, referring to **Deuteronomy 6:5**, 'Love the Lord your God with all your heart and with all your soul and with all your mind' (**Matthew 22:35-40**). In that I see the same threefold division, but here with the order of heart, will and head. Jesus is saying God wants a fully rounded, three-dimensional relationship with us. He doesn't just want to be accepted as an inescapable logical conclusion; he wants us to love him. That's important.

Now supposing some clear evidence for God was found in, say, some bizarre property of some subatomic particles. I foresee three problems.

The first is that it would be terribly exclusive: most of humanity – me included – wouldn't understand it.

The second is that such evidence for God would point to a being who was fundamentally a creator, a 'cosmic craftsman'. Of course, God is that and recognising it is a good first step to faith. But *only* a first step. After all, there have been many people who have believed in a 'someone' or a 'something' that they called the 'Supreme Being' or the 'Great Architect of the Universe' but that belief has done little to give them guidance in life or hope in death.

The third problem with such evidence for God is that it appeals to the head alone. Through it, God is, in effect, coldly and logically arguing his existence with an appeal to our reason. Faced with it, someone might grumble, 'Well, I suppose I've got no alternative but to believe in God. But I don't like the idea. I don't actually like him, but there we are: he exists.' The fact is that admiration is not affection and respect does not lead to relationship. Surely, God wants to be known as the one who, at enormous cost, has rescued us in Jesus Christ. It is only that knowledge of Christ which saves us and it is the awareness of the cross that warms our hearts into love. That's why I believe all preaching of the gospel must be focused on Christ.

Along with many people, when I look at the universe and the complexities and beauties of nature, I see pointers to God. But they remain no more than signposts, hints that suggest he exists. For the truth about who God is, what he has done for me and what he demands from me I must turn to the Bible and find Christ. In Jesus Christ, God is visible so that we can see his love for us and respond in love.

I've mentioned head and heart but let me finally turn to the issue of the will. I think God is selective in who he reveals himself to and only shows himself to those who are willing to submit to him. Faith without the obedience of the will is not true faith. After all, the devil has a profound knowledge of God (**James 2:19**) but of course opposes him. What God wants to hear are those precious words such as, 'God, I've messed up. From now on, let's do things your way!'

I believe that those who truly want to find God, and who are prepared to yield to him, will find him. I believe I have Scripture on my side. In **Matthew 7:7** Jesus says, 'Ask and it will be given to you; seek, and you will find; knock, and the door will be opened to you.' Ultimately, I think the question for those on 'the edges of faith' is not one of evidence, but whether they are willing to submit to Jesus as their Lord. That's the real challenge!

10

DO MIRACLES OCCUR TODAY?

'It's a miracle,' someone says. But what *exactly* do they mean? After all, the word 'miracle' is often used for something that is simply unexpected, unlikely or impressive: a baby, an invention or even a parking place. Far more important is the question of 'real' miracles in which God intervenes in our existence in some extraordinary and seemingly impossible way.

Many of us probably have a simple idea of how such miracles work. Let's imagine George, running late to catch a train for a critical interview. Racing to the station he says a quick prayer that he will catch the train. When he gets to the station he is delighted to find the train has been delayed five minutes and is still there. As he collapses into the seat, he gasps, 'It's a miracle.' If he thought about it, George probably imagined that God, above the world in heaven, was suddenly prompted by his prayer to reach down and act to specifically slow the train. The reality is doubtless much more subtle. For one thing, God, who knows the past, present and the future, is never surprised by events and doesn't ever operate in crisis-management mode. For another, he is not so much 'outside' events as 'inside' them. God is involved in every detail of the world, whether the death of a sparrow or the fate of one human hair (**Matthew 10:29-31**). He controls everything, everywhere in creation, all the time. This is echoed in **Colossians 1:17** where we read that Christ 'is before all things, and in him all things hold together'. On this basis, a 'real' miracle is simply an occasion where God operates in some dramatic way that catches our attention.

Miracles must be seen in the context of the fact that God has constructed the universe around what we call 'the laws of nature', which govern how the world *normally* operates. The result is that we can be confident that such things as the principle of cause and effect and the laws of properties such as motion and gravity, will not suddenly change. Were they to vary, our world would disintegrate into chaos. Would a medicine be effective? Would a recipe continue to work? Would a plane still fly? It's no coincidence that modern science arose in a Christian worldview in which a reliable God gave reality and rules.

Yet while Christians recognise a trustworthy universe, they believe that God can, and does, intervene in miracles. After all, the foundation of Christianity is that Jesus rose from the dead, and once you've accepted the resurrection, there seems little point in questioning lesser miracles. The oft-heard criticism of miracles that they break the 'laws of nature' – predictable and regular rules associated with physics, chemistry and so on – won't hold. These things are only 'laws' because we have never observed them being broken. Or, at least, *so far*. But as God makes these rules he can, as their creator, break them if he chooses.

But do miracles occur *today*? While they may not occur with the frequency and magnitude that they did in the first century, miracles do happen today. Personally, I've experienced extraordinary events, dramatic healings and answers to prayer that defy all human logic and explanation. On my *Facing the Canon* interviews I've heard many testimonies from people of events and experiences that fit the tightest definition of a 'real miracle'. And it's not just me. The scholar Craig Keener has written extensively on modern miracles giving convincing, well-documented examples in two volumes, *Miracles: The Credibility of the New Testament Accounts*, that total over 1,200 pages, and in a more accessible version with *Miracles Today: The Supernatural Work of God in the Modern World*.

Like many, I think that miracles are far more common on the 'frontline' of Christianity, where people are faced with minimal health care and open spiritual opposition. I think it's also likely that miracles are rarer in the West because we have a sceptical, anti-supernatural attitude in which we don't expect them and don't pray for them.

Although I believe in miracles today I must say that they are neither predictable nor available on demand. A recurrent theme in the Bible is the condemnation of those who, through witchcraft or sorcery, seek to manipulate the pagan gods to deliver such things as healing, children or crops. Our God is different. He is sovereign, he remains in charge and he does not dance to our tune.

We also need to remember that whatever the problems of the church, miracles are not, if you'll excuse the expression, a miracle solution. While miracles can encourage faith, they can be ignored (e.g. **John 5:1-15**) or even attributed to the devil (**Matthew 12:24**). Equally, we can let them distort our view of God, turning him into little more than the miraculous giver of what we need: a sanctified Santa Claus. Our God is more than that! We need to remember, too, that the search for the miraculous can lead down some very dark roads. Some people can pursue miracles regardless of where or who they come from, and its sobering to recall that the devil can generate miracles too (**Exodus 7:13 – 8:7**).

Let me end with two thoughts. The first is that the biggest miracle God does is conversion, in which he brings new spiritual life to those who are spiritually dead. The second is that in John's gospel miracles are called 'signs' as they point to the identity and importance of Jesus. Today, miracles continue to do just that!

11

DID ADAM HAVE A NAVEL?

Actually, the original question I was asked was 'Did Adam have a belly button?' but I thought I'd try and seek a more elevated tone. Even so, you might well be tempted to skip this as utterly trivial and jump to the next question. Yet it's a question well worth thinking about because it raises some fascinating issues.

The background here is the assumption that the Bible teaches in **Genesis 1** that everything came into being in six literal 24-hour days. Now I've discussed this in my response to Question 5 where I concluded – along with many Christians – that there is no real reason why we have to interpret those days in such a way and that, as a result, earth and the universe could be as old as the scientists want them to be.

But if you do take the view that the universe and Adam suddenly came into existence fully formed in a 'working week' then there are questions that must be asked. The issue of a man who was never biologically attached to any mother being created with a navel is simply the tip of an iceberg of issues. Did he have any memories? Did his fingernails, teeth and bones show evidence of having grown? And going beyond Adam, did the trees around him have growth rings? Did the mountains show evidence of being weathered over centuries? Did he see stars with light that had seemingly travelled for thousands, if not millions, of years?

This question of how the history of the universe related to Scripture began to surface uncomfortably in the early nineteenth century when the sciences of astronomy and geology were expanding. In astronomy, the vastness of the space and the fixed speed of light suggested the universe had to be very old. In geology, increasing studies – many done by Bible-believing Christians – revealed a long and complex history, with a seemingly endless recycling of rocks through mountain building, erosion and new sediments. Given that the belief at the time was to take **Genesis 1** as a historical and scientific account, this posed major problems. If the universe was just a few thousand years old, why did it look to be so ancient?

One answer came from the Christian Philip Gosse who in 1857 published a book called *Omphalos*, which is Greek for navel. In it, Gosse tried to solve the problem by suggesting that God had created the world in six days but looking very old. The history for the earth written by scientists was correct but it was *fiction*, not fact. Gosse, hoping to reconcile theologians and scientists, fell foul of both. Theologians felt Gosse had created a deceiving God who dealt in illusions and who, in the natural world, had created the ultimate in fakes. Scientists resented the idea that what they had taken for reality was, in fact, imaginary. Having speculated from bones and footprints how dinosaurs lived, the thought that they had never really existed struck them as ludicrous. Philosophers of science pointed out that Gosse's idea was problematic because it couldn't be tested. After all, if God had faked a world looking old, then you could presume he'd done a perfect job of it.

In general, Gosse's bright idea has left everybody unhappy then and now. Like most Christians I believe that God could have created the entire universe in a few days: he is, after all, the Almighty. But would a God who prizes truth and hates 'false testimony' (**Exodus 20:16**) really create a complex, consistent and imaginary past that never existed? Gosse's idea soon disappeared into the category of 'strange and forgotten ideas of history'. It is sometimes revived by those who believe the universe is only a few thousand years old but it's hard to uphold. While one attraction of an 'illusory past' is that it avoids the idea of God waiting for billions of years for human beings to turn up, it misunderstands the relationship between God and his creation. As God is outside time, then presumably the time in our universe is not the same for him as it is for us. It's like an author writing an account of a ten-year period in just a month. The time that passed for the creator and the time that passes in the created work are different.

Interestingly, the idea that what we see as reality may only be apparent persists outside Christianity. In recent years, the idea that we live in an 'illusory reality' has emerged amongst a number of thinkers who consider that we *may* – and only *may* – inhabit what is essentially a simulation created by some technology or intelligence beyond us. It's a minority view and, in my opinion, deserves to remain so.

Ultimately, I think to drive a wedge between belief and reality is to adopt a very dangerous strategy. Of all the world's religions (and probably philosophies) Christianity places the strongest value on physical reality. We believe God became flesh. It is no accident that science – which depends on hard, non-negotiable realities – has flourished in Christian societies. It's fascinating, too, that the resurrected Jesus wanted to demonstrate to his followers that his resurrection was not illusory and so let himself be touched and ate food. Whether Adam had a navel may be an unnecessary question, but the idea that reality is truly real is both helpful and necessary.

12

ARE WE TO FEAR GOD?

The idea that we are to fear God occurs throughout the Bible and some individuals are praised for fearing God. Today, in an age of informality, relaxation and being laid-back, fearing God seems, well, *uncomfortable*. In fact many Christians would say that it doesn't match with the New Testament image of God as our loving heavenly Father.

Whether we should fear God is important in how we relate to him. A friendly bond with our longstanding neighbour with whom we regularly relax, drink coffee and share family news is very different from a frosty connection with our distant and intimidating director at work. So when we come to God in prayer and worship, how do we approach him? In a mood of chilled-out relaxation or of troubled, nervous tension?

One way to resolve this issue is to say that the two Testaments of the Bible differ: the Old depicting God as someone to fear while the New depicting him as someone to love. For all its simplicity, this view is mistaken and misleading. Treating the Old Testament as wrong on the vital matter of how we relate to God inevitably undermines its authority. On such a view it is hard to see how Christians can value the Old Testament or how Jesus and the apostles could treat it as God's infallible word (see, for example, **2 Timothy 3:16**, 'All Scripture is God-breathed and is useful for teaching, rebuking, correcting and training in righteousness'). Another fatal problem is that not only are there many Old Testament verses about loving God (for example, **Deuteronomy 6:5**, 'Love the LORD your God with all your heart and with all your soul and with all your strength'), there are many New Testament verses about fearing him, such as Luke **12:4-5**, **Acts 10:34-35** and **Hebrews 12:28-29**. Both Testaments agree that we are to both fear and love God.

In answering this let me make three initial points.

First, 'fear' is very broad and includes such things as awe, respect, worry and terror.

Second, fear is universal. We all spend a lot of our time being subject to fears of various kinds. We worry about being burgled at home, dying young or becoming old and frail.

Third, fear controls actions. Some results of fear may be good: so electricians are wary of unknown wiring, pharmacists take precautions with powerful medicaments and vets go easy with unknown dogs. Yet fear can give bad results: a horror of criticism may prompt lies and a dread of failure lead to cheating. Fear generates many evils; after all, it drove the religious and political authorities to execute Jesus.

In **Proverbs 9:10** and **Psalm 111:10** we read that 'the fear of the LORD is the beginning of wisdom' and now let me suggest four ways in which this is indeed so.

First, the fear of God may act as a *fence for our protection*. Fear may not be pleasant but it can be helpful. I can't imagine anybody born without a sense of fear would survive beyond adolescence. And, as at a human level, fear can prevent us from trouble, so the fear of God can protect us spiritually. There are many stories – you may have your own – where a sense of fear, whether from God or of God, has deterred someone from something wrong or dangerous. Indeed there are many cases where fear prompted someone to either come to God for the first time or to turn back to him. Like sheep prone to straying we need to be kept safe, and Christ, the good shepherd, can use fear as a fence.

Second, the fear of the Lord gives a *foundation for us to stand on*. Every day, we face a fundamental question of identity: 'Who am I?' Here the fear of God allows us to recognise the awesome and potentially terrifying revelation of how we stand with our Maker. We realise that physically God is infinitely greater than us – he is the creator and sustainer of the universe, the one who controls everything on every scale from atomic to galactic, and the one who is beyond all time. Morally, we see another immense chasm. While even our best human thoughts are flawed by such things as pride, greed or selfishness, with God there is only an unmixed holy purity. This double gap would be unbearable were it not for the fact that, in Christ, God has bridged it. Yet even though we who are Christians can now know God as Father, we must not forget what has been bridged and at what cost. We can be reverently familiar with God but we can never be rudely flippant.

Third, the fear of the Lord gives a *framework for us to live by*. A second question that re-echoes through our lives is of *morality*: 'How do I live?' Here the fear of the Lord provides the scaffolding around which we can build our life. Fear includes respect and obedience. So, when faced with some temptation, we reject it saying, 'God, you know best, I will obey you,' we are expressing the fear of the Lord in the most practical way. This is why the Old Testament makes so much of God's Law as the only reliable and safe framework for life.

Finally, the fear of the Lord gives a *freedom for us to enjoy*. Because we all spend lives haunted and bound by fears, we need an antidote. Here we find that if we fear the Lord and get ourselves right with him, everything else falls into place. To fear God is to be protected by him. No one put it better than the great nineteenth-century preacher C.H. Spurgeon: 'When we fear God, we fear nothing else; when we do not fear God, we fear everything else.' The fear of the Lord is still the beginning of wisdom!

PART THREE

QUESTIONS ABOUT JESUS

13

HOW CAN JESUS BE THE SON OF GOD?

Let's get one thing clear straight away. The idea that Jesus is 'the Son of God' has many meanings but one it doesn't have – and never has had – is anything to do with 'biology' or 'sex'. Yes, amongst ancient pagans there were many lewd and lurid tales of gods engaging in 'inappropriate behaviour' with women, but in the Jewish faith even to hint that the holy and all-powerful God might stoop to this sort of conduct would be an unimaginable blasphemy. Christianity has taken the same view, and in declaring that Jesus was born of a virgin has always viewed that however God was involved in the mysterious process of his conception, it was consistent with his holy, sinless nature.

Having said what 'the Son of God' doesn't mean, what does it mean? Here we have to remember that the term 'son of', even in English, has many meanings. So, parents of an adopted boy will refer to him as 'our son', although there is no genetic link to either. Equally, we may read – perhaps in an obituary – that some man was a city's 'most honoured son'. In the Bible the sense is even wider. So for example, Jesus humorously refers to the passionate James and John as being 'the sons of thunder' (**Mark 3:17**).

As applied to Jesus, let me make five suggestions about the term 'Son of God'.

First, 'Son of God' speaks about Jesus' *divinity*. We now think of a child as the result of a blend of genetic traits from mother and father and, as such, a unique individual in their own right. It was not so in the past. Something that they didn't tell you in Sunday school is that the whole idea of conception was not understood until the nineteenth century, with the result that the male role was widely assumed to be the main, or even the only factor, in creating a child. Yes, it was a sexist view and I don't defend it, but the result was the sense that in producing a son, a man was in some way duplicating or continuing himself. So in referring to Jesus as the Son of God, there is an acknowledgement of the fact that he and the Father are a unity. This comes over in various Bible passages such as **John 10:30** where Jesus says, 'I and the Father are one'; the same idea is expressed in **John 10:38, 14:9-11, 17:21-23** and **Colossians 2:9**.

Second, 'Son of God' speaks about Jesus' *identity*. In the Bible the phrase 'son of God' is used in other contexts than Jesus and some of these are significant. Adam, for example, is made in the image of God (**Genesis 1:26-27**) and is called 'the son of God' in **Luke 3:38**. David and the line of kings from him are 'God's sons' (**2 Samuel 7:14; Psalm 2:6-7; 89:26-27**) and God's people, Israel, is considered to be the 'son of God' (**Exodus 4:22-23; Jeremiah 31:9; Hosea 11:1**). In bestowing the title 'Son of God' on Jesus we are reminded how Jesus is the perfect continuation and completion of all that Adam, David and Israel stood for and, looking forward, we see how he inaugurates a new people of God.

Third, 'Son of God' speaks about Jesus' *activity*. Here, too, we need to put the clock back. Until a few generations ago, professions were handed on from generation to generation and so it was assumed that a son would do what his father did. So in the Bible, Joseph is a carpenter (or craftsman) in **Matthew 13:55** and Jesus is also one in **Mark 6:3**. Therefore, in terming Jesus the 'Son of God' there is the recognition that in his actions, teaching and healing Jesus is doing the work of his heavenly Father (see **John 5:19; 10:37-38; 14:10**). As the saying goes, 'like father, like son'.

Fourth, 'Son of God' speaks about Jesus' *authority*. Building on the idea that a son – especially the eldest or only son – was in some way a continuation of the father, we see how Jesus bears the Father's authority. So, for instance, in traditional monarchies, in the absence or indisposition of the king, it's perfectly normal for the son to take on the authority of his father. Referring to Jesus as the Son of God here is to refer to his godly authority. That is something Jesus displays in his miracles in demonstrating his power over nature, sickness, sin and the diabolic. That authority continues after his death and resurrection as numerous passages demonstrate (**Acts 3:6-8; 16:16-18; Ephesians 1:21; 1 Peter 3:22**). Especially significant is how, as Son of God, Jesus' teaching has particular authority. In the transfiguration the voice from heaven says of Jesus, 'This is my Son, whom I love; with him I am well pleased. Listen to him!' (**Matthew 17:1-8**, see also **Mark 9:2-8; Luke 9:28-36**).

Finally, 'Son of God' speaks about Jesus' *superiority*. However you understand the term 'Son of God', the fact is that it highlights how, in every area, Jesus is bigger and better than anyone. This is made clear at the very beginning of the letter to the Hebrews where we read, 'In the past God spoke to our ancestors through the prophets at many times and in various ways, but in these last days he has spoken to us by his Son, whom he appointed heir of all things, and through whom also he made the universe. The Son is the radiance of God's glory and the exact representation of his being, sustaining all things by his powerful word' (**Hebrews 1:1-3**).

Above all, what we mustn't lose sight of is that the claim that Jesus is the Son of God is not a mystery to puzzle over but a truth that should drive us to trust and worship him.

14

WHY DID JESUS HAVE TO BE BORN THROUGH A VIRGIN BIRTH?

The 'virgin birth' of Jesus refers to the belief, expressed in every historic Christian creed, that Jesus 'was conceived of the Holy Spirit and born of the Virgin Mary'. This is separate from two other beliefs. One is the 'immaculate conception' of Mary, a belief formally stated by the Catholic Church in the nineteenth century. The other is the idea that Mary remained a virgin all her life. This is not only at odds with the many Bible texts that talk about Jesus having brothers and sisters but reflects an unfortunate view that crept into the early church, which saw virginity as superior to the married state.

The idea of the virgin birth (more precisely the 'virginal conception') is specifically taught only in the nativity accounts of Matthew and Luke. Because of its limited biblical basis, some, especially those who are sceptical about the miraculous, have dismissed it. Yet the two nativity accounts draw on very different sources and there are hints in the gospels (**Mark 6:3; John 8:41**) that there was something mysterious about Jesus' conception. Nothing in the rest of the New Testament conflicts with the virgin birth and it seems to have become a foundation of Christian belief early in the second century.

So the virgin birth has been part of Christianity from the beginning. But why was this unique event necessary? Let's take a step to the very heart of the Christian faith: that, at the cross, Jesus stood in our place and paid the price for our sins. Such a substitution demands two things: capability and eligibility. Let's imagine that we are putting together a national team for some sport. We might well make two columns for candidates: one for their capability (how good they are), and another for their eligibility. In doing so we might well find ourselves frustrated by discovering someone who would be an absolutely superb choice but who was disqualified because they didn't fulfil the requirements for nationality.

Now both capability and eligibility apply when we consider Christ's work on the cross. There has to be 'capability'. We could imagine someone who was morally perfect substituting for a guilty individual on a neat and simple one-to-one equation. Yet the problem is that, over the centuries, there are billions of people who need to be substituted for, and if Jesus was just a man, even a perfect man, that one-to-one rule applies. However, if Jesus was God, then he has the quality of being infinite, and so into the 'equation of salvation' we can add the infinity symbol. An infinite God is capable of saving an infinite number of people, including you and me.

Capable perhaps, but eligible? If Jesus was in some way only God then, if you'll excuse the illustration, you could imagine the devil standing by the cross and protesting, 'Hang on, God, you can't stand in for human beings because you're not human! You are disqualified!' But as perfect man from his conception, Jesus *is* eligible. He is one of us (**Hebrews 2:14; Galatians 4:4**).

The idea that Jesus was somehow both man and God demands a virgin birth. After all, if Jesus was not God from the moment of conception, when did he become God? At his birth, baptism or resurrection? Such options seem very problematic. The most obvious solution is the traditional one. Jesus became the unique individual he was at the point of conception.

That said, I have to observe that the virgin birth raises a number of issues, some of which are very profound.

- Traditional Christian thinking is that as the second person of the Trinity, the eternal Son of God, Jesus existed in eternity before his conception. This *pre-existence* is something supported by numerous New Testament texts such as **John 1:1-3**, **John 8:58**, **Colossians 1:15-17**, **Philippians 2:5-7** and **Hebrews 1:1-3**.

- The Bible teaches that from Adam and Eve onwards all human beings are sinful. Some people have imagined that Jesus was sinless because he had no human father. Actually, we may in fact be better off avoiding any idea of sin being genetically transmitted – and certainly just from a father – and simply consider the incarnation as a miraculous event in which a new being, a second or last Adam (**1 Corinthians 15:45**) was created.

- We read that Jesus was known as 'the son of Joseph' (**John 1:45; 6:42; Luke 2:27, 33**) and I presume that this refers to the way that Joseph would have referred publicly to Jesus as 'his son'. In **Matthew 1:25** we read that Joseph took the child and 'gave him the name Jesus', and for a man to name a child implies that he has accepted him as his son and taken legal responsibility as a father for him.

- Does the virgin birth mean that, even as an infant, Jesus had superpowers? Although we are here entering into unknown, and probably unknowable, territory, we may imagine that from his earliest consciousness Jesus was always aware he had access to powers his heavenly Father did not wish him to use and, unlike all other human beings, he did not yield to any temptation to break those limits.

- Still others have suggested that Jesus was perfect because he was God. No, Jesus was sinless because he chose to be obedient to his Father. He was subject to all the temptations we have (**Hebrews 4:15**) but, unlike us, he resisted. Jesus' perfection was due to him being good, not to him being God.

Let me end with one profoundly encouraging aspect of the virgin birth. It is that through it, God in Jesus became one with us. He is no remote, distant God, aloof and separated from the struggling humanity we are. To borrow a phrase: in Jesus, God became one of us – from womb to tomb.

15

WHY WAS JESUS BAPTISED SINCE HE WAS PERFECT AND DIDN'T NEED TO REPENT?

The baptism of Jesus by John the Baptist was clearly a significant event. It is described in the first three gospels (**Matthew 3:13-17**; **Mark 1:9-11**; **Luke 3:21-22**) and referred to in the fourth (**John 1:29-34**). Yet although every gospel writer clearly felt this was a major event, it has given rise to questions. Jesus was clearly the more important of the two individuals so why did he submit to John baptising him? Why, if John's baptism was about repentance from sins, did a sinless Jesus undergo it?

In answering these questions I think it's important to be aware that, despite similarities, John's baptism should not be seen as if it was like any modern Christian baptism.

Although the baptism that the church performed from Pentecost onwards (**Acts 2:38-41**) no doubt drew on John's practice, it was – and is – very different. Christian baptism focuses on a confession of faith in Jesus and marks an entrance into the new community of the church. What John did was something quite unique and for his time.

Although he appears in the first pages of the New Testament, John was in many ways the last Old Testament prophet. He arrived at a significant time. Much of the Jewish nation was trapped in a dull and deadly combination of formal religion and spiritual apathy, with many people assuming they were automatically accepted by God simply because they were descendants of Abraham with whom God had made a covenant. In their complacency they had no expectation that God might intervene in their day.

In his great national wake-up call, John proclaimed both accusation and announcement. He accused God's people of failing to keep their side of the covenant and announced that, without repentance, God's wrath was inevitable and imminent. With this he proclaimed the impending arrival of an individual – clearly the long-expected Messiah – who would bring with him not just redemption and the kingdom of God (**Matthew 3:1-2**) but also God's judgement. This double aspect of the coming Messiah was seen in the promise he would baptise with both 'the Holy Spirit and fire'.

The location of John's baptism was also significant. The two great events in the history of Israel were the nation's miraculous escape from Egypt through the waters of the Red Sea and their similarly miraculous entry to the promised land through the Jordan. In offering baptism through the waters, John seems to have been showing the need for a new, revived people of God. Those who underwent John's baptism were expressing their repentance and their desire for a renewed relationship with God before the coming Messiah dispensed judgement on the nation.

So given this, why was Jesus baptised by John? We read that when challenged by John on this point, Jesus said we must 'do this to fulfil all righteousness' (**Matthew 3:15**), in other words by being fully obedient to God. I think we can identify four aspects to Jesus' baptism.

Jesus' baptism marked his identification with his people. He was not personally a sinner but when he chose to undergo John's baptism, it was an expression of his unity with God's people. Christians accept that Jesus took on the sins of his people at the cross but, in fact, his identification with them began much earlier at his baptism. In fact, in **Luke 12:50** Jesus himself links together the cross and baptism as he talks about his cross as 'a baptism' that he had to undergo: he was going to be 'immersed' in suffering. This literal baptism in the Jordan foreshows the later ordeal at Calvary.

In going through the waters of the Jordan, Jesus declared himself to be one with us.

Jesus' baptism marked his submission to a calling. In 'fulfilling righteousness' by being baptised by John, Jesus demonstrated his humility and his obedient submission to God's will. He had begun the long road to Calvary. As Paul expresses it in **Philippians 2:8**, 'And being found in appearance as a man, he humbled himself by becoming obedient to death – even death on a cross!'

Jesus' baptism marked his declaration of identity. If what Jesus did at his baptism is significant, what was done to him was even more so. In Matthew's account we read, 'As soon as Jesus was baptised, he went up out of the water. At that moment heaven was opened, and he saw the Spirit of God descending like a dove and alighting on him. And a voice from heaven said, "This is my Son, whom I love; with him I am well pleased"' (**Matthew 3:16-17**). Father, Son and Spirit are united here. In the heavenly voice there are subtle references to the two great figures promised in the Old Testament: the Messiah king (**Psalm 2:7**) and the suffering servant (**Isaiah 42:1**).

Finally, Jesus' baptism marked the inauguration of his ministry. Whether it's with speeches, celebrations or formal announcements, human beings like to clearly mark the beginning of something. The baptism of Jesus marks the end of his years of silence and his emergence into public ministry. Indeed, there is a sense of a coronation here. As in the Old Testament King David was anointed king over Israel by the prophet Samuel (**1 Samuel 16**), now a far greater divine messenger anoints Jesus as king. His ministry and the kingdom of God now begin.

Why was Jesus baptised when he was not a sinner? I think the best answer is that he stood in the place of his people. Given that, it's no wonder that after his baptism, John the Baptist could say of Jesus, 'Look, the Lamb of God, who takes away the sin of the world!' (**John 1:29**). At the Jordan, Jesus became one with his people. As our Lord, he stood in our place at the cross and, God be thanked, he continues to stand with us today.

16

WHAT DOES IT MEAN TO COMMIT BLASPHEMY AGAINST THE HOLY SPIRIT?

Anybody in any pastoral ministry, especially in a church, will have come across someone haunted by the fear that they are doomed to hell because they have committed the 'unforgivable sin', something so terrible that God cannot forgive them. This may be some act such as murder or adultery, a practice such as witchcraft or even attitudes such as a hatred of God. This appalling sense of an inescapable damnation may find support in those Bible verses about an 'unpardonable' or 'eternal' sin associated with 'blasphemy against the Holy Spirit'.

The three key Bible passages are **Matthew 12:22-32**, **Mark 3:22-30** and **Luke 12:8-10**. Let me quote the 'problem' verse: 'And so I tell you, every kind of sin and slander can be forgiven, but blasphemy against the Spirit will not be forgiven.

Anyone who speaks a word against the Son of Man will be forgiven, but anyone who speaks against the Holy Spirit will not be forgiven, either in this age or in the age to come' (**Matthew 12:31-32**).

For clarity, blasphemy means deliberately abusing, mocking or showing disrespect for God. Yet given that this very passage talks about a God so gracious that he can forgive even abuse against 'the Son of Man' – that is Jesus – what *exactly* is so bad about blasphemy against the Holy Spirit?

Here context helps. In **Matthew 12:22-24** we read: 'Then they brought him [Jesus] a demon-possessed man who was blind and mute, and Jesus healed him, so that he could both talk and see. All the people were astonished and said, "Could this be the Son of David?" But when the Pharisees heard this, they said, "It is only by Beelzebul, the prince of demons, that this fellow drives out demons."' Jesus points out the foolishness of imagining Beelzebul – another name for Satan – exorcising his own demons and then in verse 28 says, 'But if it is by the Spirit of God that I drive out demons, then the kingdom of God has come upon you.' Then he gives that stern warning that 'blasphemy' or 'speaking against' the Holy Spirit will never be forgiven.

Here, it is evident that this double miracle – deliverance and healing – was an especially striking event. Jesus declared it something he had done 'by the Spirit of God' and saw it as evidence that the promised kingdom of God was at hand. Indeed, many of the ordinary people there seem to have recognised in it a sign that pointed to Jesus being the Messiah, the Son of David. In bitter contrast, the Pharisees, those who saw themselves as the guardians of the faith and who knew what we call the Old Testament in depth, took an opposing view. Had they simply treated this event with neutral, honest puzzlement, that might have been understandable. Instead, they sneeringly dismissed the clear testimony of the Holy Spirit that this miracle was from God and instead attributed it to being of the devil.

Here we see the nature of the 'unforgiveable sin'.
There are two conditions for sins to be forgiven: recognition that they are indeed genuinely sin and a faith in Christ as the one who can give forgiveness for sin. Here, tragically, both diagnosis and cure are ruled out. Despite the testimony of the Holy Spirit there is a failure to acknowledge personal sin, and Jesus is treated not as God's *saviour* from sin, but as the devil's *agent* of sin.

Here we see that blasphemy against the Holy Spirit is not primarily an act, gesture or words but rather a deliberate and contemptuous attitude that scorns God and denies both sin and salvation. To blaspheme against the Spirit is to reject his testimony and his call to accept grace. There is a grim, terrible logic here: to reject God's offer of salvation in Christ must inevitably result in eternal loss.

Let me address two related questions.

First, can a Christian commit the unforgivable sin? This is linked with whether believers can lose their salvation. Personally, I find it impossible to believe that anyone who has undergone a genuine conversion and has, as a result, been given the gift of eternal life (**John 3:16**), been adopted into God's family (**Ephesians 1:5**) and become indwelt by the Spirit (**1 Corinthians 3:16**) can ever commit this. But please, note that word *genuine*. It's worth remembering too that a characteristic of blasphemy against the Holy Spirit is to be unconcerned to the point of contempt about spiritual matters. So if someone is troubled that they might have committed the unforgivable sin then that very concern suggests that this sin is not one they have committed.

Second, what if we have some friend or relative whom we believe has committed this sin? Is all hope lost for them? Here I'm inclined to say that while blasphemy against the Holy Spirit is the unforgivable sin, I see no evidence that it is final. I believe that, like all sins, people can repent and come to faith even on their deathbed. Pray on! Where there's life, there is hope.

Finally, in grappling with these hard words of Jesus, let's not overlook the glorious phrase 'I tell you, every kind of sin and slander can be forgiven'. *Every kind!* The history of Christianity is full of men and women who did appalling things, repented, turned to Christ and received forgiveness. The great biblical example is of course Saul, with his history of brutally persecuting Christians and approving the stoning of Stephen (**Acts 8:1**), who became Paul the great apostle. We need to hold onto the fact that ultimately, as every page in the New Testament states, the focus of the gospel is not the grim news of eternal judgement but rather the joyful news of deliverance from it.

17

WILL PEOPLE BE CONDEMNED FOR NOT BELIEVING IN JESUS EVEN IF THEY'VE NEVER HEARD HIS NAME?

In answering questions like this, one Bible verse is essential. 'The secret things belong to the LORD our God, but the things revealed belong to us and to our children forever' (**Deuteronomy 29:29**). It's a reminder that while there are clear truths to find and obey, there are limits to what we can confidently know. In thinking about this question we are inevitably going beyond God-given certainties into areas where we can only speculate.

In *Will I Be Fat in Heaven?* I looked at the question 'Do all religions lead to God?' and this takes that further: if Jesus is the only way to be saved from eternal judgement, will someone who has never even heard of him go to hell?

Before we proceed into any speculation let's remind ourselves of some certain biblical principles.

- All human beings are guilty before God. Everyone has some awareness of a creating and caring God and his rules for life (**Romans 1:18 – 3:20**). Yet, sadly, every human being has broken whatever moral system they follow.

- Our sins have created a gap between us and God, and unless we are forgiven that gap will have an eternal dimension, with us being separated from God and from every good thing *for ever* in the tragic and terrible state that is hell.

- In his love God has created a way for that separation to be ended through Jesus. On the cross, Jesus – perfect man and perfect God – paid the price for those who, through faith, are his brothers and sisters. The cross is a bridge over that great gap of separation. But note: it is the *only* bridge.

- The only way to God is to trust in Jesus and obey him. In **John 14:6** we read, 'I am the way and the truth and the life. No one comes to the Father except through me' (see also **Acts 4:12; Romans 5:1-2; 1 Timothy 2:5-6**).

Because no other religion offers either such a profound analysis of the human problem or such a perfect antidote to it, Christ is our world's only hope. So what happens to those who've never heard of him?

In responding to this question we must always keep in mind the two great aspects of God's character. First, he is righteous: 'Will not the Judge of all the earth do right?' (**Genesis 18:25**). Second, he is loving. We can read not only the famous verses about 'God is love' (**1 John 4:8; 4:16**) but also **Exodus 34:6**: 'The LORD, the LORD, the compassionate and gracious God, slow to anger, abounding in love and faithfulness.' So I believe anybody troubled about the eternal fate of someone who never understood the gospel, either due to some mental disability or their death in infancy, can rest confident in the never-ending love of God.

With regard to Old Testament believers who lived before Jesus, we see that with Abraham – 'the father of all who believe' – his faith was enough to make him righteous (**Romans 4:11-12**). A saving faith in Old Testament times was not a matter of rituals and keeping the religious law but having a trust in a loyal and loving God, confessing personal sin and being aware that this represented a debt before God. Of those who trusted in the sacrificial system to pay that debt, many no doubt sensed that it must point to something far more effective and lasting. Ultimately, Old Testament believers were saved, not by keeping the Law, but by the Christ who, when he came, finally fulfilled it.

I won't repeat what I said about hell in my previous book. It is, however, worth mentioning the idea that there might be 'gradations' within hell. Because God is a God of justice, judgement will be fair. In **Luke 12:48** Jesus says, 'From everyone who has been given much, much will be demanded; and from the one who has been entrusted with much, much more will be asked.' In his elaborate imagining of hell, the medieval poet Dante put 'good pagans' in an outer circle that, while being far from the blessings of paradise, was free from pain. *Perhaps . . .*

In considering someone who has not heard the gospel, let's imagine a 'best case' scenario: an individual who believes in one creator God, has held to a high morality, but who, aware that they have failed to keep it, has thrown themselves on God's mercy. Here I find it conceivable that God may accept such a person through the Jesus they have not heard of. One model for this in Scripture would be the story of Cornelius in **Acts 10** who was clearly seeking God and, in Jesus, found who he was seeking.

That said, I'm afraid such individuals are probably rare. The problem with other religions is not just that they don't present the answer in Jesus but that they don't present the problem either. Instead of encouraging any hunger to be right with God they deaden it, dismissing it as meaningless, offering idols as protection or pretending that sacrifices will ease any guilt. Unfortunately, you need to know the bad news before Christianity becomes good news.

Even if there may – and only *may* – be a glimmer of hope for those who are outside Christianity, they are still in deepest darkness. They have no certainty of salvation, no knowledge of God as a loving Father and no presence of the Spirit. In summary, they have no help in life and no hope in death. They need to hear the gospel.

Actually, in my experience this question is more frequently an excuse than a genuine objection. Ultimately, for all of us, the big issue is not speculative questions of how God acts in eternity but whether *we personally* have taken Jesus as our Saviour. Let's not get preoccupied with veiled mysteries for others when we must deal with vital certainties for ourselves.

PART FOUR

BEING MADE RIGHT WITH GOD

18

DOES EVERY HUMAN BEING HAVE A SENSE OF RIGHT AND WRONG?

Behind this question lies a challenge: is God unfair? Let me explain. The Bible is clear that all human beings have broken the rules of a holy God and are therefore sinners. This uncomfortable verdict is stated by Paul in **Romans 3:23**, 'All have sinned and fallen short of the glory of God,' but is supported elsewhere in the Bible (see **Psalm 14:3**; **Proverbs 20:9**; **Ecclesiastes 7:20**; **Isaiah 53:6**). While this harsh view jars with the comforting modern sentiment that human beings are fundamentally good, it fits with the flawed state of the world. This bleak analysis of humanity before God explains why the forgiveness offered through Jesus is called good news.

Here, however, comes the challenge. Although everybody is judged guilty, have we all been given the rules? In a sports contest it would be considered unfair if competitors were disqualified for breaking rules they were unaware of. The Christian would say that the rules for life are to be found in the Old Testament Law with its summary, the Ten Commandments (**Exodus 20:1-17**), and that these were reaffirmed by Jesus in the Sermon on the Mount (**Matthew 5 – 7**). But can't those who have never heard of these plead ignorance in their defence?

Paul, a pioneer in preaching to non-Jews, discusses this challenge in **Romans 2:12-15**. He writes that everybody is accountable to God, whether they know the Jewish law or not: 'All who sin apart from the law will also perish apart from the law, and all who sin under the law will be judged by the law' (**Romans 2:12**). He then says of the Gentiles, who do not know the law, that they are 'a law for themselves' and that 'the requirements of the law are written on their hearts'. Paul is stating here that not only does everybody have some sort of moral system but it's one that they fail to keep.

The extent to which all humans have a moral system and are aware of right and wrong has been much studied. I believe two things are clear. Not only does everybody have a general moral awareness but also, beyond this, human beings make – and aspire to keep – specific moral codes.

A *general* moral awareness with some imprecise sense of right and wrong seems to be universal. In every culture, people judge others, condemn behaviour that is bad and, less frequently, praise that which is good. The reaction of everybody to some insult or theft is to say 'that's not fair' or 'it's not right'. By doing so we are applying values of right and wrong. This ability to decide what things are right and wrong seems to be 'hardwired' into human beings and has been demonstrated in infants only a few months old. Although this general morality is somewhat vague, a profoundly significant feature is that however we define our own standards of right and wrong, we inevitably break them ourselves. 'Do as I say, not as I do' seems to be a universal feature of human beings. When we point a judging finger at someone, there are three fingers pointing back to ourselves. We are indeed a law to ourselves.

If everyone has a general moral awareness about things being right or wrong, can we say the same for *specific* moral standards? Let's take the Ten Commandments. Are these also built into the human brain? Not in a precise sense it seems, but there is strong evidence that all men and women hold to some common universal values. So everybody values generosity, empathy, courage and hospitality, and upholds values such as setting some limits on sexual desire, respecting what others own, helping family, group or community and sharing resources fairly. Anthropologists have found that the so-called Golden Rule of Jesus, 'Do to others what you would have them do to you' (**Matthew 7:12**), is universally recognised; indeed many cultures have a similar ideal. That such specific moral values exist across the world is demonstrated by the global success of many Hollywood films. Everywhere, people want the good character to triumph, the villain to be punished and justice to be done. And with these specific moral standards we find the same phenomenon as we did with the general awareness of morality. Whatever codes we agree to, we end up breaking.

Of course, what specific values are held and how tightly varies. So some cultures may prioritise honour over telling the truth and others put loyalty to the community above other values. Furthermore, specific moral values can change. So, for example, most of the world no longer approves of slavery. The shift of moral values is, however, not always in a good direction and is one reason why we Christians use the Bible to calibrate our own values of right and wrong.

A related question is whether we are all judged equally severely by God. Imagine two people: one raised in a firmly moral environment and the other in a rough, tough setting where lies and theft were endemic. Now imagine that both steal an identical sum of money. The crime may be the same, but is the sin the same? Here, as elsewhere, the principle spelled out by Jesus in **Luke 12:48** surely applies: 'From everyone who has been given much, much will be demanded; and from the one who has been entrusted with much, much more will be asked.'

I believe that everybody has not only some sort of general moral awareness but, in addition, a specific, more focused moral code. Although there are variations due to such things as culture, background and mental ability, the striking point is that whatever moral code we have and with which we judge other people, we fail to keep it. We are laws to ourselves and stand judged by how we judge other people. Every one of us is a sinner and we all need God's forgiveness in Christ.

19

DO WE CHOOSE GOD, OR DOES HE CHOOSE US?

The careful reader of the Bible will find two seemingly contradictory positions on how we are saved by Christ. One view is that our salvation depends on our own personal choice and the other is that it depends on God's choice. These serious differences deeply affect our outlook on our Christian faith.

Let's step back first to remind ourselves that to become a Christian is to receive salvation, to be 'saved'. In the New Testament, you find that salvation is actually a set of interlinked gifts. I just list them here but all are worth investigating and contemplating. So, to be saved by Jesus Christ is to be forgiven by God and to be adopted into God's family so that we can now know him as our Father. It is to become a member of the new people of God, the church, and it is to receive the gift of the Holy Spirit, to be liberated from the devil's authority and to be given the promise of eternal life. To accept Christ is to be given a whole new life overflowing with blessings and privileges! How do we gain this fortunate situation? It is by *confessing* we have fallen short of God's standards, by *repenting* of our sin, by *trusting* in Christ and his death on the cross and by *accepting* Christ as our Saviour and our Lord. This would, I think, be agreed by all Christians who take the Bible's authority seriously. Yet there is a serious disagreement over the role that God and human beings play and here we must go into some theology.

One part of the Protestant church, the Reformed or Calvinist branch, emphasises that ultimately our salvation is due to God's decision, not ours. Men and women come to faith in Christ because God has chosen them or, in biblical phrases, 'predestined' or 'elected' them to come to faith. On the Reformed view, if you are a Christian, it is not because you chose Christ but because God led you to seek Christ. Such a view has much support in Scripture. So in **John 6:44** Jesus says, 'No one can come to me unless the Father who sent me draws them, and I will raise them up at the last day.' In **Ephesians 1:4-5** Paul writes, 'For he chose us in him before the creation of the world to be holy and blameless in his sight. In love he predestined us for adoption to sonship through Jesus Christ, in accordance with his pleasure and will.'

In contrast is the Arminian view which places the responsibility for salvation firmly on human choice. Here we are saved because, out of our free will, we chose Jesus. Here again there are biblical verses in support. So, for instance, **Revelation 3:20**, 'Here I am! I stand at the door and knock. If anyone hears my voice and opens the door, I will come in,' and **Deuteronomy 30:19**, 'This day I call the heavens and the earth as witnesses against you that I have set before you life and death, blessings and curses. Now choose life, so that you and your children may live.' Other verses cited in favour of the Arminian position are **Joshua 24:15** and **1 Timothy 2:3-4**.

Both views have their strengths and weaknesses.
The Reformed view emphasises God's sovereignty over events and people. Yet the Reformed position seems to make human free-choice an illusion and, by implication, makes God responsible for people who are not saved. It also raises awkward evangelistic questions: is the person we are sharing the gospel with actually one of the elect chosen by God? And, at a church level, Calvinism can lead to complacency in evangelism.

In contrast, the Arminian position upholds the importance of an individual's choice and encourages preaching with an appeal to faith. Yet it too has problems. It suggests that God is somehow powerless unless an individual believes, and that seems to go against the biblical picture of a God supremely in charge of history. It's also very difficult to see how it can overcome the many biblical texts about God's sovereignty in preaching. So in the book of Acts we find: 'When the Gentiles heard this, they were glad and honoured the word of the Lord; and all who were appointed for eternal life believed' (**Acts 13:48**).

In fact, many Christian leaders and preachers stand back from taking a hard-line view on either position. First, being on the front line of the Christian faith, we have better things to do than scratch our heads over seemingly irresolvable contradiction. We are practitioners, not professors. Second, God has blessed Christians on both sides of this divide. So, in the eighteenth century, the Arminian John Wesley and the Calvinist George Whitfield respected each other, cooperated in ministry and both saw thousands saved.

Actually, these contradictory positions may not be as irreconcilable as it seems. After all, with normal vision, our right eye and left eye see different images yet, merged in the brain, they allow us to see in three dimensions. And modern physics knows many cases where seemingly contradictory positions are considered to be true. In salvation we deal with matters that this side of heaven, we may not be able to understand.

Do we choose God, or does he choose us? I'm helped by the following old illustration. There is a great entrance that leads into the Christian faith and as you approach it as a non-Christian you see inscribed above the doorway, the command, taken from **Revelation 22:17**, 'Whosoever will, may come!' Yet having taken the step of faith and gone through, if you look back as a believer, you see written on the inside of the door a statement drawn from **Ephesians 1:4**, 'You were chosen before the foundation of the world.'

Where these issues do have an intense practical importance is in the question of whether in fact we can lose our salvation. But that's the next question!

20

CAN I LOSE MY SALVATION?

In my previous answer I outlined the privileges of salvation: forgiveness, adoption by God, the gift of the Holy Spirit, spiritual liberty and, ultimately, heaven itself. But can you lose all this? After all, some who profess Christianity end up denying it. Sometimes there's an outright rejection of Christian morality or beliefs but often just a slow, unspectacular slide into something that is no longer real Christianity.

Whether believers can lose their salvation is a hotly discussed topic in Christian circles. To deal with it I must refer to those different theological positions – the Reformed (Calvinist) and the Arminian – that I talked about in Question 19.

The Reformed position, often summed up in the phrase 'once saved, always saved', is that no genuine believer can lose their salvation. There is logic here: the sovereign, all-powerful God who began salvation will see it through to the end and those brought to true faith in Christ will arrive safely in eternal glory. Paul expresses this sequence of salvation in **Romans 8:30**: 'And those he predestined, he also called; those he called, he also justified; those he justified, he also glorified.' In support are many other passages such as **Philippians 1:6**: 'He who began a good work in you will carry it on to completion until the day of Christ Jesus.' We need to remember, too, what Jesus promised his followers, 'I give them eternal life, and they shall never perish; no one will snatch them out of my hand' (**John 10:28-29**, see also **John 6:38-40**). In the Reformed view, God holds the believer so securely in his hand that neither the devil nor they themselves can rip them away.

The Arminian view is that Christians can indeed lose their salvation. This, too, has its own logic: as an individual chooses, out of free will, to join the Christian faith so, on the same basis, they can choose to leave it. In support of this position are various Bible verses such as **Colossians 1:22-23; Hebrews 6:4-6; 10:26-29; 2 Peter 2:20-22** as well as Jesus' warnings that his followers could fall away (see **Matthew 24:10-13; Mark 4:16-17; Luke 8:13; John 15:6**).

Here, as in the previous answer, both positions have strengths and weaknesses. With the Reformed view the believer has the wonderful assurance that they are held safe by God, something that is an enormous help in life's struggles. Yet this view faces challenges. How does it explain those who, having professed faith, have left it? Here one Reformed answer is to say that such people weren't genuine children of God but had merely an appearance of faith. Yet this raises the troubling question as to how *any* believer can know whether their faith is authentic. Another answer is to suggest that such people are indeed genuine born-again believers and that, before they die, God will somehow bring them back to himself. Another concern with this Reformed view is that it can encourage a spiritual complacency. After all, if arriving at your eternal destination is guaranteed, why bother to live out your faith?

The Arminian view lays emphasis on avoiding any spiritual carelessness and on working hard at the Christian life and faith. Yet it carries a nagging uncertainty for any believer. Under trial or temptation, might we too depart from the Christian faith?

On balance, I prefer the Reformed 'once saved, always saved' view. As I have noted, salvation is not simply signing up to a set of beliefs, it is to undergo a radical, life-changing spiritual transformation – a new birth – with profound consequences. Were it possible for such an overwhelming conversion event to be reversible, I would expect to see much more evidence of it in Scripture. Yet I find no threats that the gift of the Holy Spirit might be withdrawn from the Christian, their new birth reversed or their status of forgiveness in Christ revoked. Above all, I see no evidence that the loving God who has adopted us into his family might eject us from it. Parents don't do that.

In conclusion let me make several points.

First, in terms of philosophy or theology, we need to recognise that there are enormous issues here to do with God and eternity that we are probably not able to resolve. Humility, caution and tolerance are essential.

Second, all those who know Christ can trust that God's hold on them is greater than their hold on him. Linked to this is the reassurance that we have a God of grace who is ready to offer forgiveness to all who need to turn – or perhaps *return* – to him in true repentance.

Third, although the Reformed and Arminian views differ markedly in how the faith works *in theory*, there is very little conflict in how it works *in practice*. Neither view offers comfort to those whose Christianity is in name only and both encourage serious commitment to living out the faith. On the Reformed point of view the believer needs to practise the Christian life in such a way as to demonstrate that they are indeed a true child of God. So, in 2 Peter 1:10 we read, 'Therefore, my brothers and sisters, make every effort to confirm your calling and election.' From the Arminian perspective the believer needs to make every effort to stay firm in the Christian faith. The result of this similarity in how Christians live means that many churches, organisations and indeed entire denominations have got along well for years despite having members with very different views on this topic.

Ultimately, our confidence depends on having been given 'the Spirit of adoption' (**Romans 8:15-16**). Proof that we have this indeed is given by a life that is filled with the fruit of the Spirit: 'love, joy, peace, forbearance, kindness, goodness, faithfulness, gentleness and self-control' (**Galatians 5:22-23**). The best way to be reassured that you are a brother or sister of Jesus is to show a family likeness!

21

WHAT DOES IT MEAN TO HAVE FAITH IN CHRIST?

Christians speak much of the importance of faith. We are, we say, 'saved by faith' and can quote many Bible verses in support: for example, 'For it is by grace you have been saved, through faith' (**Ephesians 2:8**) and 'Know that a person is not justified by the works of the law, but by faith in Jesus Christ' (**Galatians 2:16**). Yet what exactly is meant by what we might call 'saving faith'? After all, it's not uncommon to meet people who say 'I have faith in Jesus Christ' but clearly do not have anything that gives them guidance, self-control, hope or peace. So what does having 'faith in Christ' mean?

Saving faith must be based on Jesus. The sad fact is, however, that many people put their faith in someone or something other than humankind's only Saviour, the Jesus of the Bible. So some people have faith that their good actions will put them right with God. Others have a faith in which they have conjured up a God or Jesus so generous and tolerant that he condones all they've done or are doing. Some have faith in their church or its rituals to see them safe into eternity. Still others seem to have faith in faith: the view that as long as you believe in *something*, that's all that counts. *No*. The Bible is clear that only Jesus can save us (**John 14:6; Acts 4:12; 1 Timothy 2:5**).

Now, in thinking about 'saving faith' it's helpful to recognise that there are three different types or levels of faith. Let me describe them.

First, there is a 'one-dimensional' faith which is no more than a mental agreement to some facts: it is a 'faith of the head'. So someone may say, 'I believe Jesus existed and was who he claimed to be.' Yet if there is nothing more than this, it's hardly a biblical or saving faith. In fact the Bible speaks of this sort of faith and considers it utterly inadequate. So although the Pharisee Nicodemus says he believes that Jesus is 'a teacher who has come from God' (**John 3:2**), Jesus still tells him that he has to be 'born again' (**John 3:3**).

Second, there is a deeper 'two-dimensional' faith where, in addition to a mental agreement, there is an emotional response such as gratitude or hope. This is a faith of the head *and* heart. So someone may say, 'I have faith in Jesus, I recognise he died for me and I'm comforted by thinking that he will receive me into heaven when I die.' Now, if those words are matched by a consistent Christian life then that may well indeed be a genuine saving faith. But without such evidence, they may simply indicate that very perilous state in which someone has a false and fatal confidence that everything is right between them and God.

Third, deepest of all, there is a 'three-dimensional' faith and it is this kind of faith that the Bible speaks of. Here there is not just mental agreement and emotional response but also action. It is a faith of head, heart and will, and is best described in the word *trust*. Let me give an example. One-dimensional faith believes that hang-gliding is safe; two-dimensional faith goes further to consider it as exhilarating; but it's only the three-dimensional faith of trust that will have you leaping off a cliff. It's precisely this sort of three-dimensional head, heart and will faith we need to be saved. We need a faith that constantly seeks to work itself out in obedience and practice.

Let me list six marks of this authentic, saving, three-dimensional faith in Christ.

- ***Conscience.*** Is there an awareness of sin and the need for repentance, not just at the start of the Christian life, but throughout it? Is there a sensitivity to the prompting of the Holy Spirit?

- ***Commitment.*** Is there a dedication to Christ and to his people that is above all other loyalties? This may be shown both in our refusing to do what is wrong and choosing to do what is right.

- ***Communion.*** Is there a life that revolves around God? Is there a pleasure in Bible reading and prayer? Is there a knowledge and love of God in Christ? It's important to remember that true faith centres not on a *thing*, but on a person, Jesus Christ.

- ***Cost.*** For Jesus to save us cost him everything. In what sacrificial way do we respond to that supreme act of grace?

- ***Change.*** Is there a transformation? Has Christ's influence through the Holy Spirit altered our life? The test here is surely the listing in **Galatians 5:22-23** of the 'fruit of the Spirit'.

- ***Continuation.*** Has our faith lasted and endured, not just through the good days, but also through the bad ones?

In short, to repeat an old challenge that has not lost its relevance, 'If Christianity was a crime, would there be enough evidence to convict you?'

I accept that these are demanding tests and could lead many people to question whether or not they have indeed got that trust in Christ that counts as saving faith. First, let me point out that these marks of true faith are not mine but those of the Bible itself. Second, let me remind you that we come before a God of grace and forgiveness, our heavenly Father. In **Matthew 12:20**, quoting **Isaiah 42:3**, we read these encouraging words about Jesus: 'A bruised reed he will not break, and a smouldering wick he will not snuff out.' Ultimately, to have faith in Christ is to put your trust in the good shepherd who cares for even the weakest of his sheep. True faith is to trust him and stay close to him!

PART FIVE

GOD AND GOD'S WORLD

22

DO GHOSTS EXIST?

Ghosts intrigue many people, are a preoccupation for some and a source of anxiety for others. But are they real?

Let's define a ghost as 'the appearance of a dead person to the living'. When someone has a personal vision that no one else can see, is that a ghost? Surely, a ghost is more: an objective, 'real' appearance that, in theory, could be seen by several observers or recorded on video.

Ghosts and ghost stories are incredibly popular. Sceptics argue that the obsession by Hollywood and the media with the 'paranormal' encourages people to see unexplained events in such supernatural terms. Others would say that our fascination with ghosts and the supernatural today is a rebellion against the all-embracing technology of our time.

Do ghosts exist? Let's consider the view from both science and Christianity.

At least publicly, science is deeply sceptical towards ghosts. Scientists are troubled by the fact that it's impossible to do laboratory experiments on ghosts and the frustratingly poor quality of the data on them. Understandably, when faced with a ghost few people choose to investigate closer. There are, too, logical issues with ghosts. If they are insubstantial 'spirit' creatures, how do they wear clothes and how do they speak? Sceptical scientists also propose alternative explanations, particularly where the encounter is confined to one individual. Some point to the many tricks the mind can play, such as the *déjà vu* experience of having a confident familiarity with someone or somewhere you have never before seen.

One other mental trick is *pareidolia* where we see patterns in such things as cloud shapes or rock formations. Science also points to the possible influence of fever, drugs or drink or, with the recently bereaved, the influence of grief and trauma. A powerful piece of evidence for sceptics is that, although for many years now people have carried phones capable of taking good photographs and video, there remains a remarkable lack of authenticated imagery of ghosts.

Many Christians, particularly those who take the Bible seriously, are also cautious about ghosts. Although the cultural setting of the Bible was one in which people believed in ghosts, we find little in the pages of Scripture that affirms them. Those who seek ghosts and spirits are condemned in **Deuteronomy 18:10-11** and in **1 Samuel 28:7-20**, when the desperate King Saul has a medium summon the dead prophet Samuel, it is unclear whether the subsequent apparition is actually Samuel. It's notable that the resurrected Jesus says he is not a ghost and proves it by eating food and being touched (**Luke 24:37-42**). A strong Christian objection to the idea of ghosts as the returned dead is that there is no 'spiritual niche' for them. The New Testament is clear that there are only judgement and heaven or hell for the dead (see **Hebrews 9:27**) and the idea of any deceased individual 'lingering around' is ruled out.

So with scepticism from science and suspicion from Christianity, the case against ghosts seems firm.

And yet. The idea of ghosts is universal, occurring in every global culture, past and present. Today, statistics suggest that 40 per cent of Britons and Americans believe in ghosts. That a view is popular is, of course, no guarantee it's true. But these are striking figures. We must also remember that science does not know everything about everything, and in fact the universe is turning out to be a very unpredictable place indeed. And no Christian, with their belief in God, miracles and the resurrection, can deny a supernatural dimension to the universe.

So are ghosts real? It's undeniable that people have *experiences* that they consider to be ghostly encounters. What lies behind these, however, is less clear. Perhaps a better question is, 'How should we approach the idea of ghosts?'

This is an area where Christians should keep a safe distance. At very least it is a distraction. Christians are no exception to the attraction of the spectacular but our priority as believers is not seeking out sensational supernatural activity as 'Ghostbusters for Jesus' but the much less dramatic – and far more vital – matter of loving God and our neighbour.

In fact this area of supernatural manifestations may be a real danger. Although I am hesitant on ghosts, I have no such hesitancy about supernatural powers that are evil, and sometimes subtly so. There are too many stories, some well attested, of those whose curiosity and naivety led them down dark paths that ultimately betrayed them. An often-used image here sees the supernatural world as a spiritual zoo in which there are fierce and deadly creatures that, by virtue of Christ's triumph, are locked away in cages. Blundering around may result in those cage doors being opened with unfortunate consequences. Now, there are those Christians, probably in church leadership, who may, out of duty, be called on to battle with supernatural manifestations of our enemy. But it's not something that the curious or amateur should stray into. If you do find yourself in some unsought encounter with ghosts or the like, then it is important to remember that the only source of victory over them is our relationship to Jesus Christ who, at the cross, triumphed over 'powers and principalities' (Colossians 2:15; Ephesians 1:19-21).

Finally, as an evangelist, let me point out a fascinating feature of supernatural manifestations which is that an encounter with them can force an individual to look beyond the closed, arid world of scepticism to God himself. To be so scared by a ghostly experience that you run into the arms of a heavenly Father may seem an awkward way to come into the kingdom of God. Nevertheless, it's the destination you arrive at, not how you are brought there, that counts.

23

CAN I BELIEVE IN EVOLUTION?

I find it troubling that some Christians are more likely to get worked up about the age of the earth or whether evolution took place than about how to live holy lives, feed the starving or witness to their friends. There's a desperate need in the church to ensure that the main things remain the main things.

Evolution is a hot topic so in thinking about it, I've picked the brains of Christians who are professional scientists. The result is the recognition of three separate and very different ideas of evolution which should not be confused. Let me call them Evolution 1, 2 and 3.

Evolution 1: This can be summarised as *'The small-scale genetic shift of organisms over time.'* This is microevolution. It has been observed in both the laboratory and nature in everything from viruses to birds and, given that it allows organisms to adapt to changing environments, is an essential process. It is clearly scientific, a proven fact and has no conflict with Christianity.

Evolution 2: This can be summarised as *'The gradual emergence of all living things through an unbroken succession from a common ancestor over several billion years.'* This is 'geological' or 'historical' evolution: the idea that, over countless generations, something like bacteria have progressively developed into all the complex multicellular plants and animals of our world. This definition of evolution is still science but not 'observational science': it happened in the past and cannot be tested in the lab. Nevertheless, the integration of vast amounts of data on fossils with DNA studies has given a generally consistent account of how plant and animal groups developed over time.

Although this Evolution 2 is simply a description of events and says nothing about an ultimate cause, some might say it conflicts with religion. For a start it seems to replace God's supernatural action by *chance*. But if you take the view, generally associated with Calvinism but in fact thoroughly biblical, that God oversees every event in the universe, then there is no such thing as real chance; it's only apparent. (Note **Proverbs 16:33**, 'The lot is cast into the lap, but its every decision is from the LORD.') Interestingly, God's control of natural selection whereby 'unfit' animals or plants are removed is anticipated in Jesus' comment in **Matthew 10:29**: 'Are not two sparrows sold for a penny? Yet not one of them will fall to the ground outside your Father's care.' The fact that an event can be both natural *and* supernatural is something we take for granted. So when a child recovers from a deadly infection, we don't see any conflict between the doctor's report that the antibiotics worked and the parent's gratitude to God that their prayers were answered. A view of God working to bring the natural world into being through this strictly defined evolution could be termed either *Theistic Evolution*, *Guided Evolution* or, my preference, *Continuous Creation*.

For the Bible-believing Christian I think there are three issues here. The first is whether the Creation account in **Genesis 1** demands six literal 24-hour days, something I discussed in Question 5, where I concluded otherwise. The second is whether it conflicts with **Genesis 1**, and here I would suggest that this is only the case if you see the Bible's statements as some sort of scientific text. The third is how it fits with the scriptural emphasis that human beings are made in God's image and thus, in some meaningful way, separate from the animal kingdom. Well, the physical links between humanity and the animal world are undeniable: humans and chimpanzees have something like 95-99 per cent of DNA in common. Nevertheless, the gulf between humanity and even the highest apes remains enormous. We alone have complex language, possess analytical thought, make advanced tools, have intricate social structures and engage in complex rituals. One image that may help is to remember that although a desktop computer today may look broadly similar to one built thirty years ago, it is enormously more powerful in its ability and potential. In the same way, although we have similar biological 'hardware' to other apes, it could be said that God has given us vastly different and much more powerful mental 'software'.

Evolution 3: This can be summarised as *'Evolution is the only creating force in the universe. It is the mechanism through which all things have come into being. There is no supernatural God or higher powers, only evolution.'*

Although rarely put so starkly, it is this view that underlies most of the many problems with the word *evolution*; here normally capitalised as Evolution and sometimes termed Evolutionism. It is a philosophical view of the purpose or mechanism behind the universe. Indeed, precisely because it pronounces – negatively – on the existence of God, it is a religious opinion and based on faith. Of course this is in total opposition to Christianity or indeed any other religion.

So where does this leave us? The limited microevolution of Evolution 1 gives no problems, whereas the third definition has nothing but problems and can instantly be rejected. Cautiously expressed and thoughtfully understood, the 'historic evolution' or 'continuous creation' of Evolution 2 seems reasonable. But in discussing it, we must always make clear our belief that running through it all is the supervising hand of God.

In making these definitions let me point out a trick, employed by sceptical atheists, which is to say that because Evolution 1 is proven and Evolution 2 is probable, therefore Evolution 3, *Evolutionism*, automatically follows. It doesn't.

Can a Christian believe in evolution? My cautious verdict is that, carefully defined as an account of how God has worked, it's a reasonable position. What is much less reasonable is for the non-believer to see the glory of the natural world and attribute it all to nothing more than the interaction of time and chance. The beauty and wonder of the creation point us to a creator.

24

WHY DID GOD CREATE MOSQUITOES?

Mosquitoes are a nuisance far out of proportion to their tiny size. It's easy to have some otherwise perfect summer meal with friends ruined by their whining nastiness, and although some people seem immune to mosquito bites, others suffer for days. Of course, the problem with mosquitoes is far more serious than irritating bites. They carry diseases and in taking blood from us can, in return, share bacteria, viruses and parasites – notably, malaria. It's been estimated that each year around 700 million people acquire a mosquito-borne illness, with over 725,000 deaths as a result. With this comes a vast economic damage due to lost productivity.

Some facts first. Mosquitoes are a family of small flies with a four-stage life cycle. Almost all of the 3,500 named mosquito species feed on plant nectar but in about 200 the females suck blood to give them protein to help make eggs. The problem for humans is that, in stopping our blood from clotting, the mosquito pumps in saliva with an anticoagulant. As well as triggering those immune responses that result in the familiar irritation and swelling, this saliva may carry diseases.

In answering why a good and wise God created mosquitoes let me first point out some positives about them.

Mosquitoes are truly extraordinary organisms. So, for instance, the notorious mosquito whine is because their wings beat between 450 and 600 times *a second*. From the point of view of mechanical engineering, that's astonishing. No less remarkable is the way they sense the presence of humans, even selecting blood type (they prefer O) and gender (they prefer pregnant women). You may not like mosquitoes, but you've got to admire them. We Christians may struggle with them as the product of a good God but any thinking atheist should puzzle how such super-sophisticated organisms can be the product of nothing more than that ruthless formula of 'time and chance alone'.

Furthermore, mosquitoes play an important role in the amazing interlocking machinery of nature. Many animals, including birds, bats and fish, feed on them and the aquatic mosquito larvae take up organic waste, some of which is harmful. In addition, let's not forget that mosquitoes can teach us. They are astonishing flying machines that make aircraft seem clumsy. They have amazing sensory abilities, take blood samples almost painlessly and produce superb anti-clotting agents. There's lots we can learn from them.

Ultimately, however, faced with this and similar questions, I think three big responses are needed.

First, *theological reflection*. An important element in Christian thinking is that, in a way we do not fully understand, this world is not what it was intended to be. It is fallen. Some Christians hold that this fallenness is the result of the rebellion of Adam and Eve a few thousand years ago. Those who respect the scientific consensus of an earth billions of years old – in which blood-sucking mosquitoes have been preserved in amber from the time of the dinosaurs – often postulate a much earlier 'cosmic fall' that affected creation. This may be what Paul refers to in **Romans 8:22** in talking about the 'whole creation' groaning 'as in the pains of childbirth'. Was there a warping and twisting of the natural world that goes back to the fall of Satan himself? We don't know – we haven't been told.

Second, *thorough reverence*. As our Lord and creator, God is perfectly within his rights to refuse to give us an answer. After all, if we knew the answer to every question we would, in effect, be like him. As **Deuteronomy 29:29** reminds us, there are secret things that belong to God. At the end of the book of Job, which focuses on why the innocent Job suffers, God speaks. What is fascinating is that he doesn't actually give Job any explanation. Instead, the thrust of God's message seems to be 'I am the Lord God, you are merely human and a bit of humility will not go amiss'. It's a useful lesson.

Finally, *thoughtful response.* Sometimes our questions to God can boomerang back. We ask theoretical questions about such problems as mosquitoes, poverty, floods and earthquakes and I think any answer from God comes with the sharp riposte, 'Yes, it's a problem. *Fine*. So what are *you* going to do about it?' After all, we must not neglect the human role in making the damage done by mosquitoes so severe. Reductions in mosquito-borne diseases could be easily achieved by improved sanitation in poor areas, providing free mosquito netting and health-care systems with cheap drugs for treatment and prevention. I have no doubt that if humanity devoted a fraction of what it spends on warfare to combating mosquitoes, the damage done by them would be enormously reduced.

Let me offer here one fascinating and challenging response to a similar problem. The gruesome Guinea worm is a parasite which grows within the human host until finally, up to a metre long, it emerges through the skin with appalling pain. In 1986 it affected an estimated 3.5 million people in twenty-one countries in Africa and Asia. About then Jimmy Carter, a Christian, former peanut farmer and a man who had just vacated the White House as President of the United States, decided to make his mission in life not just to reduce the impact of the Guinea worm, but to *eliminate it totally*. Largely through education, his Carter Centre has, at the time of writing, almost totally succeeded. A mere fourteen cases were reported worldwide in 2023 and, thanks to Carter's determination, the worm is now on the verge of extinction.

Yes, like so much that is evil in the world, mosquitoes pose challenges for Christians. Yet paradoxically, they also offer enormous opportunities for doing good and for demonstrating Christian love in action. That's always the best answer to evil!

25

WAS GOD RESPONSIBLE FOR COVID?

In dealing with the COVID pandemic, we must tread delicately. Although for many it was no more than a weary, wasted year of frustration, fear and far too much screen time, for others it was a time of bitterest tragedy. It also raised complex medical and health issues, and the extent to which human beings were responsible for the beginning and spread of the pandemic is still debated.

A reminder of the facts. The COVID pandemic was caused by the highly contagious SARS COV-2 virus which attacks the human respiratory system, sometimes severely enough to lead to death. Emerging in China in early 2020, the virus spread round the world in months, causing probably between 10 and 20 million deaths and striking severe blows to the economy, society and mental health. As the virus evolved and vaccines took effect, the pandemic waned and was declared over by the World Health Organization in May 2023. It is, however, important to note that the virus has not gone away and continues to evolve.

Let's here try to answer a first question: was God responsible for COVID? Here matters are complicated because there was certainly some human involvement and responsibility. So it seems likely that the transmission of the virus into humans occurred when some wild animals, perhaps bats or pangolins, were eaten as food. There is little doubt that the spread of the virus was enabled by the inadequate reaction of various medical and government services.

Yet above these human factors stands the God of the Bible – sovereign, all-powerful and all wise – who, to use the modern term, 'micromanages' the universe. Indeed the way that a tiny virus wreaked such havoc across the world demonstrates exactly why God has to micromanage things. So God must have been involved in some way with the spread of COVID. Probably the wisest thing is to avoid such simplistic language as 'God made the virus' and instead say that he *allowed* it.

But *why*? That's the inevitable follow-up question. Let me suggest three possible responses – and do note that they are not mutually exclusive.

One response is that we must view COVID as a *mystery of God*; an event where his purposes defy our comprehension. This is hardly unexpected. An implication of having a God who is infinitely wiser than us is that, by definition, we are unable to fully comprehend all his actions. We see life as a board game on which we are playing draughts; the reality is that God is playing chess, and probably in at least three dimensions. While there is undoubtedly much truth in this view of COVID as 'mystery', the fact is that it feels unsatisfactory.

Another view is that the pandemic was a *judgement by God*. But on exactly who, or what, was it a judgement? If it was supposed to be on a specific community or individuals then there was, to use the phrase, an appalling amount of 'collateral damage'. It's also worth remembering that what we can call 'judgement' may simply be the automatic result of human wrongdoing or stupidity. Is it 'judgement' if a careless electrician gets electrocuted for neglecting to turn the power off before working with wires?

If indeed the pandemic was due to the reckless eating of wild animals then the judgement was perhaps focused on the human tendency to treat the created world as no more than a resource to be looted, abused and, in every sense, consumed. Another focus of judgement might be the laziness, folly and neglect that prevented effective management systems from reacting as they should.

Perhaps a more promising view is to see COVID as an event in which there were *reminders sent by God*. Through

COVID, God reminded us of three things that we often bury under our preoccupations of activity and pleasure.

First, in COVID we were reminded about *our true vulnerability*. Each of us was brought face to face with the fact that, within days, we could die. This is an important reminder in an age when most people operate on the principle that they are immortal. We need to recognise that our days are limited and so make the most of them. And, of course, we need to prepare for eternity. At the level of society and nations, God reminded us of the fragility of those structures of healthcare, commerce and administration that we take for granted. One message echoing through the various reports on COVID now emerging is the necessity of building 'resilience' into such structures.

Second, we were reminded about *our true values*. COVID made us appreciate much we took for granted: conversations with friends, shaking hands, having hugs, countryside walks. We saw how valuable families and friends were. We learnt the value of solid, careful medical science and careful, thoughtful and courageous decision. And, in contrast, we saw the triviality and inadequacy of so much political posturing and evasion.

Third, we were reminded of *our true vision*. Most of us rush through life in 'crisis management mode', never giving any real thought about what we are doing with our lives.

The enforced pause that COVID inflicted on most of us, offered us the opportunity to think about our actions and ambitions.

Why did God send COVID? While I see elements of both mystery and, in some way, judgement, I think there was also a wake-up call in reminders over who we are, what we are doing and what we are working for. As COVID hopefully retreats into history, we need to ask ourselves what we learnt from the lessons God sent with it. After all, it's a universal wisdom that if you are given a lesson and don't learn from it, then beware. It may be repeated.

PART SIX

GOOD AND EVIL

26

DO ANGELS EXIST?

The topic of angels suffers equally from the sceptical who will believe nothing about them and the credulous who will believe anything, however weird. Of the various ideas about angels in popular thinking, I'm only going to deal with what you might call 'biblical angels'. After all, the only reliable knowledge we have about angels comes from the 300 references in the Bible. Any doubts about the existence of angels should be resolved by how Jesus frequently refers to them in the gospels.

The Bible nowhere defines angels but takes them for granted, with the result that we have to piece together a picture of who they are and what they do. I've given the briefest summary here but to do justice to angels, you have to sit down with a Bible and a systematic theology book and consult the various references.

One false, if common, belief about angels that we must reject is that they are the souls or spirits of the dead. No!

Angels are immortal, supernatural creatures created by God at the dawn of creation. Although spiritual beings, they can take on a form solid enough to allow them to speak and to move things: they rolled away the stone at the resurrection of Jesus. The Bible speaks of the heavenly realms being occupied by an uncountable number of angels: the 'angelic host'. It also indicates there is a diversity and hierarchy within angels, with 'archangels', 'cherubim' and 'seraphim'. Some angels have names: we know of Gabriel and Michael. Although angels are beings with intelligence, the Bible's emphasis is more on their ability to serve than their wisdom or insight. They faithfully transmit God's message; they don't interpret it.

Angels are normally invisible but can take on human form. In a few cases they are described as having wings – but that may be symbolic language referring to their ability to travel anywhere rapidly. It is widely assumed that angels are supremely beautiful but I find little evidence for this. In fact the way angels are often initially mistaken for human beings suggests that, on earth at least, they may be very ordinary in appearance.

The focus of the Bible's treatment of angels falls on how they relate to humans and here there is a clear separation between us and them. Although we lack the power, immortality and holiness of angels and their privilege of seeing God, we human beings are superior in important ways. We are made in God's image, are loved by him and, at enormous cost, have been redeemed by him in Christ. Although there are rebellious angels, there is no mention of God redeeming them.

A misleading belief about angels is to consider them as cosy, reassuring beings. They may be, but coming from the very presence of God as his faithful servants and carrying his divine authority, they can be bearers of death and judgement. In the Bible the appearance of an angel is often enough to bring terror to a human being and it's common for an angel's first words to be 'Don't be afraid'.

Angels need to be treated with respect and wisdom. They cannot be worshipped. Neither should they be sought. If we want to deepen our faith, we should not pursue angels but, through his word, God – Father, Son and Spirit. We also need to be aware that some 'angelic manifestations' may not be from God but from the devil. There are numerous sad accounts of people being led astray by lies they believed had come from angels, but no angel can contradict what God has revealed to us in the Bible.

So what do angels actually do? In summary, they have three roles.

First, *angels praise God*. Simply by their existence, the 'angelic host' gives God glory. On earth it's common for the majesty of monarchs and leaders to be enhanced by an entourage or noble figures around them. Similarly, the presence of millions of angels adds to God's splendour and majesty. Furthermore, angels are not simply a silent presence in heaven. From the Psalms and elsewhere in the Bible, we learn that they continually give God praise.

Second, *angels proclaim God's message.* In both Hebrew and Greek the word translated as 'angel' means 'a messenger'. While God can speak to people in dreams and visions he can also use angels.

Third, *angels protect God's people.* Angels use their power and authority to guard and support God's people. Although there's not much evidence for the popular belief in 'guardian angels' in the sense of each of us having an attendant angel, there's a lot of evidence that angels protect God's people.

In all three roles of praising, proclaiming and protecting, angels provide encouragement for Christians. So, for instance, we can be encouraged to praise by the thought that our feeble worship is joined with that of the angels. And in our proclaiming of the gospel, angels set us an example in their bold and authoritative presentation of God's truth. In terms of protection, angels are a tremendous encouragement for Christians at times of trial and threat: we are not alone. Yet, equally as angels defend and protect God's people, so we should be those who guard our brothers and sisters in Christ.

Do angels appear today? It's notable that in the Bible, angels tend to appear at critical moments or crises in the history of God's people. So we find angels at Jesus' birth, his crucifixion and resurrection. But in our time? It's not easy to say: after all, angels work without drawing attention to themselves. And of course, today Christians have the power and presence of the Holy Spirit; a blessing which, in some ways, makes much of the proclaiming and protecting work of angels unnecessary. But, personally, I think angels are an unseen and unappreciated presence around us, particularly in times and places of intense spiritual conflict. But I have heard of so many people who have seen them, including several friends, so yes, they can appear and I hope I will see one too. Thank God for angels!

27

IS THERE A DEVIL?

Despite the horrors of the modern world, many people remain sceptical about the devil. This is doubtless encouraged by his cartoon appearances in a scarlet cloak and with horns, tail and pitchfork. Some people suggest that the devil is no more than a personification of some inbuilt human tendency towards what is wrong. Yet given how much malice, hate and evil occurs in the world and how it is often worked out in savage and furious ways, many other people sense the need for an explanation in terms of a *someone* rather than a tendency.

Christians have no choice but to acknowledge the devil or Satan. Jesus and the early church treated him as a real being, and if they are wrong here how can they be trusted elsewhere? As in the previous answer on angels, I shall ignore many varied and bizarre beliefs and limit myself to what the Bible teaches.

In pursuing the subject of the devil in the Bible, it is notable that although the Old Testament mentions angels and is frank about the existence of evil, it says little about the devil. The mysterious serpent in the Garden of Eden is unidentified and the figure of 'Satan' only emerges in three places – **1 Chronicles 21:1**, **Job 1 – 2** and **Zechariah 3:1** – where he is an angelic accuser. Significantly, it is only with the coming of Christ into the world as the great victor over evil that the idea of the devil or, as he is often named, Satan, comes into focus. The New Testament also reveals that the serpent in Eden was the devil himself (**Revelation 12:9; 20:2**).

Something that cannot be overemphasised is that, despite the damage he does, the devil remains no more than an angelic being. He was created by God, but rebelling against him, is now only an evil or 'fallen angel'. Satan's fall is told as a 'flashback' in **Revelation 12:7-9** and may be hinted at in the account of earthly kings in **Ezekiel 28:11-19** and **Isaiah 14:12-14**. As to how evil came into the universe, the best speculation is that the creation of a universe in which free-will was possible, inevitably meant that rebellion was possible.

Whatever his origins, Satan is the prince of the powers of evil (**Matthew 9:34; Mark 3:22; Luke 11:15**) who attack God, his creation and his people. Possessing unrelenting hate and malice, the devil is a murderer and a liar (**John 8:44**). His influence is so extensive that Paul can say that Christians struggle not 'against flesh and blood, but against the rulers, against the authorities, against the powers of this dark world and against the spiritual forces of evil in the heavenly realms' (**Ephesians 6:12**). Elsewhere Satan is referred to as the 'prince of this world' (**John 12:31; 14:30**) and the 'god of this age' (**2 Corinthians 4:4**).

Nevertheless, for all the recognition in the New Testament of the power of the devil, Christ is everywhere depicted as the victor over him. We see how the devil repeatedly tries but fails either to destroy Jesus or tempt him from his path. We see, too, that Jesus claims authority over evil in his teaching and demonstrates it in his exorcisms, his healings and, supremely, in his triumph over Satan's ultimate and most terrible weapon, death itself. Indeed, the message of the gospel in Acts, the letters and Revelation is of the glorious victory of Jesus and *with him* his church, over all the devil is and has done. Jesus shared in our 'humanity so that by his death he might break the power of him who holds the power of death – that is, the devil' (**Hebrews 2:14**). In **Colossians 2:15** Paul says of Jesus that 'having disarmed the powers and authorities, he made a public spectacle of them, triumphing over them by the cross'. (For other verses on this topic see **1 John 3:8** and **Revelation 12:10-11**.)

The New Testament picture is then balanced on the subject of the devil: matching his menace with the truth that he is defeated and his destruction assured.

Let me sketch five helpful responses to the devil.

***Realise* the reality.** We need to be aware of Satan as our 'enemy' who is like a 'roaring lion looking for someone to devour' (**1 Peter 5:8**). Yet his powers are limited by God himself so that the devil is, in effect, a chained lion.

***Refrain* from that which is risky.** A wise response to the devil is not to put yourself in harm's way. Every Christian has some weaknesses. Identify yours and avoid those areas of life where you will be at particular risk.

***Resist* temptation.** When faced with the attraction of doing something wrong, remind yourself that the devil lies and never delivers what he promises. Remember, too, that temptation is always limited in time and force. We are told in **1 Corinthians 10:13** that there is always a way out. Ultimately, we must stand our ground (**Ephesians 6:10-17**).

***Remember* your relationship to Christ.** Part of the strength of being a Christian is that we do not face the devil alone. In the power of the Holy Spirit, we stand in Christ, the victor over the devil.

Finally, *rejoice* in the coming victory. For the Christian, it's important to remember that our battle against the devil is limited. It will not go on forever. One day, either by us going to Christ or him coming to us, we will be safely beyond the devil's power. *Forever*!

28

CAN WE BELIEVE IN THE RETURN OF JESUS?

The return of Jesus is a complex and conflicted topic and I can only cover a few aspects here.

The return of Jesus (the 'Second Coming') is not something that can be removed from Christianity. In the Old Testament, there is the frequent hope of the 'Day of the Lord' when God's people would be finally rescued and their enemies judged. In the gospels, we find Jesus building on this and talking about his return in majesty (for example, **Matthew 24 – 25**; **Mark 13**; **Luke 21:5-36**; **John 14:3**). Almost every page of the rest of the New Testament mentions the return of the Lord Jesus. It's also worth noting that every ancient creed of the church refers to Jesus coming again to judge the living and the dead.

So, putting aside debatable matters, let me offer a 'bare minimum' view of Christ's return. At some point in the future, possibly only days and weeks away but quite conceivably not for hundreds of years, history will be abruptly interrupted by the arrival of Christ. His appearance will be unannounced, glorious, universal and physical, and will set in motion what are called 'the last things'. So, Jesus will be declared globally as Lord, the devil's reign will be ended, the Last Judgement will reward the saved and condemn the lost and, finally, the glorious, eternal kingdom of God will begin.

Opinions differ as to whether Jesus can return at any time or whether there are signs that must be fulfilled first. Personally, although it raises questions, I believe it is safest to believe that Christ could appear at any moment.

Perhaps the biggest issue Jesus' return raises is how we can conceive of a sudden transformation of a universe that seems so ancient, vast and solid. In fact this 'solidity' is merely apparent. Almost all of what we consider to be reality is in fact empty space. And if you think of those glimpses of heaven in the Bible (e.g. **Genesis 28:10-12; Isaiah 6:1-4; Acts 7:55-56; Revelation 4 – 5**) they can easily be thought of in terms of some temporary insertion into our world of some different dimension. In an age where people habitually talk about a multiverse with numerous universes, it's not hard to imagine that, as Christ returns, the 'universe of heaven' completely invades and transforms our own flawed and fallen one.

Let me make three brief suggestions about how Christians should hold to the truth of Jesus' ultimate return.

First, Jesus' return should be a *primary belief.* For all its difficulties and the way it has been a magnet for strange ideas, Jesus' return must be central to our faith. Without it, nothing is satisfactorily resolved: evil remains and the world remains a mess. Furthermore, the idea that there's another, far better, world ahead is a powerful antidote to the seductive attractions of the world around us.

Second, Jesus' return should be a *protected belief.* For all its importance, the Lord's return can be distorted. One way is how, despite Jesus' warning that the date of his return is hidden, attempts can be made to predict it. Another is to treat the return of Christ as some mental theological puzzle rather than the believer's deeply longed for 'blessed hope'. Another risk is how a fascination with 'end time' events can ignore their morality, with the result that every environmental disaster or horror in the Middle East comes to be greeted, not as a matter for lament, but as another welcome tick of the countdown clock to Jesus' return. Still another risk is how a focus on a return of Christ within a very few years can discourage creating such things as Christian hospitals, universities, schools and even Bible translations that demand a timescale of decades or even generations.

Finally, Jesus' return should be a *prized belief.* The return of Christ will bring both justice and glory. For the believer, all that is wrong, in every way, will be finally and fully resolved. Those miseries, mistakes or 'might-have-beens' will be ended and mended. *Hallelujah*!

Can we believe in the return of Jesus? Yes! And we can join in John's words at the end of Revelation: 'Amen, come, Lord Jesus'!

29

HOW CAN WE WAGE WAR ON PEOPLE WHEN WE ARE SUPPOSED TO LOVE EVEN OUR ENEMIES?

War is terrible. It also poses particular challenges for Christians in view of both the teaching of Jesus and his example of submission to injustice at the cross.

Let's give some biblical background. At the beginning of the Old Testament we have the great statement that all human beings are made in the image of God (**Genesis 1:26-27**); on that basis they need to be treated with respect and dignity. Elsewhere in the Old Testament we see two repeated themes. One is the hope of peace, *shalom*, while the other is the uncomfortable recognition that evil operates in the world and must be resisted. The Old Testament also recounts those uncomfortable 'holy wars' – matters I covered in *Will I Be Fat in Heaven?* Christians agree that the conditions for these no longer apply today: there are now no nations who are God's covenant people and so there can be no 'holy wars'.

The teaching of the New Testament is not merely negative about violence but positively celebrates peace and forgiveness. Followers of Jesus are to love their neighbours (**Matthew 22:36-40; Romans 13:9-10; James 2:8**) and, in the Sermon on the Mount (**Matthew 5 – 7**), are taught to be peacemakers, to resist evil and to love their enemies. In the Lord's Prayer, Jesus insists on forgiveness (**Matthew 6:12**).

For Christians and others, war raises other problems. It disrupts and destroys everything that is good, whether that be development, education, culture or the natural world. It is incredibly costly: a single modern fighter jet costs as much as a mid-size hospital. It is also dangerously corrupting: by breeding hate, suspicion, secrecy and dishonesty, wars can turn even the noblest cause into something evil. The nineteenth-century German philosopher Frederick Nietzsche wrote, 'Beware that, when fighting monsters, you yourself do not become a monster.' Many wars, begun with noble intentions but ending in savagery, have demonstrated the truth of this.

But how, if we are supposed to love even our enemies, can we fight them? We need to remember here that the biblical definition of love is not an emotion but the desire and action of doing good to someone. To love your enemies is to act in their best interests.

Here we need to recognise that we exist both as individuals and as members of a community such as a family, a town or a nation. As individuals, when we personally are faced with wrong, I believe we should seek to forgive and to reject vengeance or retaliation. Yet we do not exist alone. We are all linked to other people; we have a responsibility to our 'neighbour'. While we might be 'personal pacifists' about evil done to ourselves, we cannot take the same approach when harm is done or threatened to others. Let me give an obvious example. Walking home at night you come across someone being beaten up. Morality demands action; to continue past would be to fail to show love to the victim. Should your words fail, that might mean physically intervening, something that could result in harm to the perpetrator. You could argue that to break up the fight is actually showing love to the perpetrator by reducing their wrongdoing. Whether ultimately they stand before a human judge or God himself, they will be greatly helped by having to admit to nothing more than inflicting bruises.

This principle of reluctantly intervening to protect others from harm forms at a national level the rationale for military action. Out of love – albeit a tough love – we may have to stop people who want to do evil to others.

We need to be brutally realistic here. Not everything that is wrong in the world can be resolved with conferences and resolutions. There are those who delight in doing evil and in the last quarter of a century it's become clear that because much evil is not based on reason, no amount of empathy, pleading or discussion can stop some violent action. As the lesser of two evils, forceful intervention may be necessary to prevent a greater harm being done.

Although the history of the church is far from blameless – the Crusades are a particular stain – warfare has troubled Christians for over 2,000 years. There has long been an honourable pacifist element within Christianity but, in general, a consensus exists that, in a fallen world, force may be necessary.

One element in Christian thinking that has been accepted beyond the church is the 'Just War Theory' – the *just* here being in the sense of justice. This sets down the principles for going to war. These include the need for any war to correct a serious evil, be a last resort and have a probability of success. Just War Theory also sets down limits on carrying out a war: it should be directed towards combatants, not civilians; the military force used should only be what is necessary; excessive violence and cruelty should be avoided;

prisoners of war should not be mistreated. It's easy to criticise Just War Theory. It has no legal force, many – perhaps most – modern wars have broken its guidelines and it fails to handle how to respond to a terrorism in which war is never formally declared by a state. Yet it's better than nothing and Christians should insist that such principles are kept.

Christians can, however, go further than simply accepting guidelines that do no more than limit warfare. Wars do not arise from nowhere but come from those who stir up hatred or let injustice occur. Christians should seek to identify the roots of conflict and try to remove them. Equally, where conflict has occurred they should aim to build bridges and restore peace. 'Blessed are the peacemakers, for they will be called children of God,' said Jesus (**Matthew 5:9**). And that surely means that we who are children of God should be peacemakers.

30

WHY ARE CHILDREN BORN WITH DISABILITIES?

The issue of children born with disabilities is no abstract philosophical or theological conundrum to be coolly debated; it is one of profound personal experiences full of anguish, disappointment and sorrow.

There are three responses to this question: the medical, the theological and the practical.

First, the *medical response*. There are a wide range of disabilities that babies can be born with: a missing or malfunctioning organ or part of a skeleton, a condition such as Down's syndrome, or many other conditions. To a greater or lesser extent, science largely understands what's happened and why. So some disabilities are due to inherited genetic factors, cell division errors or spontaneous gene mutations, and others to exposure to some medications, alcohol, tobacco, drugs or industrial chemicals. Still other defects may be due to particular infections, to radiation such as X-rays or to the health, diet or age of the mother.

And, although childbirth is vastly safer than it ever was, it's a complex event that can result in some disabilities.

In the vast majority of cases, these are things that 'just happen' and *no one is to blame*. Of course, as any health professional will tell you, the use of drugs or alcohol in pregnancy does increase the risk of having a child with a disability. But there's a long-standing temptation to try to explain disabilities by pinning blame or guilt on something or someone, and it's almost always wrong and unhelpful. Finally, it is important to have a sense of proportion. The remarkable fact is not the number of children born *with* disabilities but the number born *without* them. Something like 97 per cent of babies arrive without any disability. Given that in a mere nine months the two cells involved in conception have multiplied to around 26 billion cells, this is astonishing.

Second, the *theological response*. What must be rejected is the belief that such afflictions are the punishment for wrongdoing. This idea of some cause-and-effect link between sin and suffering is as old as the human race. It's addressed – and countered – in the Old Testament book of Job, but centuries later we meet it when Jesus' disciples assume that a man was born blind due to either his sin or his parents' (**John 9**). It's a link that Jesus denies. The reality is that because of the human race's rebellion against God, this is a fallen world where things are not as they are supposed to be and where sickness, suffering and pain can happen to all. Infant disabilities are just one particularly sad element of our world's sorry state. Nevertheless, we can also hold on to the hope that one day this world will be gloriously restored. In the gospels we see how Jesus healed many people with disabilities, and one of the best ways of thinking about those miracles is to see them as a foretaste of the glorious future for God's people. In heaven, as **Revelation 21:4** promises, there will be no more pain, suffering or death.

As to whether God is 'responsible' for infant disabilities, the issues are fundamentally the same as those I discuss in answering the question about COVID (Question 25). We must accept that, at the very least, God allows such things to happen. Human beings, however, play their part and as a result many of the medical causes of infant disability can and could be reduced. Genetic counselling can minimise the transmission of inherited disorders, environmental factors can be decreased and risks in childbirth minimised by better healthcare.

One theological point of enormous practical importance is the Bible's teaching that all human beings are created in God's image (**Genesis 1:27**) and, as such, have infinite worth and dignity. This needs to be constantly affirmed because the view that babies with disabilities are 'disposable' is never far away. Such a view is common in many cultures, was brutally practised by the Nazis and is still proposed today by some. No!

Finally, the *practical response*. A priority in any Christian response to children with disabilities is an intelligent and sustained love. For all the splendid affirmation of disability in such things as the Paralympics and the increasing availability of disabled access at venues, there is still a long tradition of keeping children with disabilities 'out of the public eye'. This must be resisted. It is worth remembering that anyone who lives long enough will acquire disabilities: it's called getting old.

Our compassion also needs to be one of long-term commitment. A vice of our age is *tokenism*: brief or symbolic gestures of support that may look good but achieve little. So when faced with something like a birth disability, we can simply express the appropriate sentiments, make some small one-off donation and then forget about the matter. The reality is that those who have children with disabilities may need support, not just for days or weeks, but for decades. Indeed, some of the most challenging circumstances are where ageing parents are struggling to care for their children who are now adults with disabilities.

I believe how we treat those with disabilities is a key indicator of the spiritual and psychological health of ourselves and our communities. In Matthew 25:31-46 Jesus says that ultimately the authenticity of our Christian faith will be shown by how we aid (or ignore) those suffering individuals that he calls 'the least of these'. Infants born with disabilities are surely in that category.

While it may be challenging to explain why infants are born with disabilities, there is no challenge in knowing how to respond to such cases. Let's drop clever answers from the head in favour of caring action from the heart!

PART SEVEN

LIFE AFTER LIFE – THE FUTURE, HEAVEN AND HELL

31

WHAT WILL HEAVEN BE LIKE?

The only reliable information we have on heaven comes from the Bible. Yes, people claim they have had visions of heaven and there are accounts of 'near-death experiences', but we must question whether they reflect eternal reality.

If the Bible gives us definitive information, it is, however, limited. The Old Testament says little about life after death and it's the New Testament that tells us most, but here we must peer through symbolic language. Heaven is described as a place of feasting and drinking (**Matthew 8:11; 22:1-14; Luke 13:29; 14:15**) and a wedding banquet (**Matthew 25:1-13; Revelation 19:7-9**). Now I like both parties and weddings but I'm sure that heaven is more than an eternal food-fest. What we surely have here is symbolic language for a culture, familiar with hunger, in which there was nothing better than being with friends and family around a food-filled table. Beyond these references we see the promise of fulfilment, fellowship and joyful celebration.

Popular thinking imagines heaven as some sort of frail and insubstantial universe with its inhabitants drifting around as misty, ghostly forms. That's wrong. When he was resurrected Jesus was very solid, and as he is 'the first fruits of those who have fallen asleep' (**1 Corinthians 15:20**) both the occupants of heaven and their dwelling place must also be substantial. In fact, it's helpful to realise that heaven cannot be *in any way* less than this world. No one there is going to long for shopping, the Internet or Premier League football.

Why doesn't God tell us more about heaven? Well, he doesn't have to. As creator, God has the right to choose what he does and doesn't reveal. **Deuteronomy 29:29** tells us that 'the secret things belong to God'. One possible reason is that heaven may be beyond our understanding. After all, even if we could talk to a baby in the womb, we would be unable to communicate anything meaningful about what walking around in the open air involved. I don't think anybody would be helped if God had told us that heaven involved 'a multi-dimensional, extra-temporal, transpersonal existence' even if we understood what the words meant. Another possible reason for our limited knowledge is that it may be for our own best interest. Our duty at the moment is to walk daily along the road of the Christian life and not have our eyes so focused on our ultimate destination that we trip up on the obstacles lying just before us. The Bible is not a handbook on heaven for future residents, but a route map to get us there.

What is heaven like? Let me cautiously offer some answers.

Who will be present? The New Testament is clear: the central person of heaven is Jesus Christ in whom we will see God 'face to face' (**1 Corinthians 13:12**). The book of Revelation offers us several images but whether as the 'King of kings', the 'Lord of lords' or 'the Lamb who was slain', the focus is Christ.

Many talk about heaven as if it was primarily going to be some great family reunion. (Those who have experienced dysfunctional families and warring marriages are here less enthusiastic.) Actually, although the renewal of human relationships in heaven seems assumed, the Bible makes little of it. Given that we will be with the redeemed of every race and culture (**Revelation 7:9-10**) the emphasis seems less on us meeting those we know than us meeting those we don't. And above all, the focus of heaven will be our Lord Jesus, in all his glory.

What will be present? There will be peace, joy, hope, beauty and music in unlimited amounts. Furthermore, **Revelation 21:24** and **26** promise that the splendour, glory and honour of the nations will be present. I imagine that all that is good and honourable in human culture will be present. Indeed, I think among the many themes of heaven will be restoration and fulfilment. We can imagine that those good things in this life that were lost will be found, those that were broken will be mended and those that failed will triumph. Above all, there will be free, authentic, genuine and glorious worship of God – Father, Son and Holy Spirit.

What will be absent? The blessings of heaven will include some absences. The devil and his angels will have been destroyed and, with them, all sin. So there will be no hatred, anger, greed, dishonesty or lust. With their abolition, the residents of heaven will be able to be who they really are and, better still, who they were meant to be. The more subtle forms of sin, such as pride, apathy, ignorance and stupidity, will also go. As **Revelation 21:4** promises, I see a welcome ending to all grief, shame and regret. I suspect we will have either the erasing of memories or the healing of them.

One joy will be an 'ending of endings'. Whereas even the best moments and meetings in this life end, they will not do so in heaven. There, all that is good will grow, expand and multiply forever. Ultimately, all and every darkness of this life, will be swallowed up in the light of eternity with Christ.

These words are utterly inadequate to describe heaven. I suspect there we will repeatedly hear awed words along the lines of 'I never imagined it was going to be as good as this!'

Just make sure you are there.

32

WILL THE EXISTENCE OF HELL SPOIL THE JOY OF HEAVEN?

In my previous answer I tried to describe what heaven would be like and I hope you had a sense of the joy, wonder and celebration that will abound. But in considering heaven, a question has often been raised. How can the saved rejoice there while somewhere – inevitably one thinks of *below* – the lost are suffering in hell? Here, borrowing ideas from others and again with caution, let me offer some suggestions.

I don't like talking about hell. I covered it – with reluctance – in *Will I Be Fat in Heaven?* Let me remind you that however much we dislike the idea of hell, the fact is that the Bible – and Jesus in particular – talks about it. Even allowing that some of the language about hell is symbolic, it is clear that it is some sort of real and appalling destiny. To dismiss hell as some outdated, mistaken and exaggerated image is to concede that Jesus was wrong about the afterlife. That's too high a price to pay. I think we must keep the idea of hell, but that doesn't mean accepting every popular image and myth about it. So, for instance, the devil is commonly portrayed as the master of hell; in fact he suffers in it.

Let me suggest that, from the perspective of this life, there are two problems about hell.

First, there is the general objection that in the eternity of heaven, hell would be some sort of moral atrocity. Imagine you arrive at some allegedly wonderful five-star beach hotel in a beautiful location, only to find that next to it was a detention camp overflowing with appalling suffering. It would spoil your holiday. Wouldn't hell have the same effect on heaven?

Second, there's the personal objection that it's hard to see how anybody could enjoy heaven knowing loved ones were in hell. How can we be joyful with a friend or relative in hell? Let me broaden this issue.

In trying to pull together some of the responses to these problems, let me start by reminding you that we know and understand very little about eternity or the final state of the lost. Many of our speculations may be badly wrong. It's also worth remembering that no one can say, with absolute certainty, that any particular individual is in hell. Deathbed conversions can occur – remember the account of the thief on the cross (**Luke 23:39-43**) – and equally, who knows what can happen in those mysterious moments of death?

I live in hope that many people observed defiantly boarding the train for hell did in fact get off before it reached its final destination.

One way of helping us over these objections is to remind ourselves that there is a logic and even a justice to hell. Ultimately, sin is the rejection of God's loving rule for us; it is to say to God, 'My will, not yours be done.' On that view hell is an inevitable consequence in which God says, in effect, 'You have chosen to live your earthly life without me. Very well, I respect that choice – I will leave you alone for all eternity.' That may sound fairly harmless until we remember that every good thing, such as peace, joy, friendship and forgiveness, is a gift from God. In hell, separated from God, there can be no good thing. One of the most chilling absences in hell was highlighted by the medieval Italian poet Dante, who imagined that above its grim doorway was inscribed, 'Abandon all hope, ye who enter here.'

Other suggestions have been made to ease 'the problem' of hell. Some have proposed that in heaven we will have a selective memory so that the lost, or even the idea of hell itself, will be erased from our minds. I struggle with this. I see heaven as a place of truth, not deception and not somewhere with a horrible secret lurking in the basement. It is also notable that in the parable of the rich man and Lazarus (**Luke 16:19-31**), the rich man in hell is able to recognise someone up in heaven. So surely the reverse works and those in heaven must see hell? Equally, the idea that in eternity we will thank God for our salvation demands we will have some memory of who we were and what we were spared from. Even allowing for some healing of memories it seems difficult to see how we can remember our past with important individuals erased from it.

There are other suggestions, some perhaps more helpful. One is the idea that in heaven we will be so taken up with the overwhelming glory of God – Father, Son and Holy Spirit – that any dismay over the existence of hell or any grief over particular individuals will be overcome. A related proposal is that in eternity, heaven will expand and grow while, in contrast, hell will shrink to the point that with time it becomes insignificant, almost to the point of non-existence.

I said at the start that there were problems with hell from 'the perspective of this life'. The fact is that our perspective in our rebellious and fallen state is distorted and only in heaven will we see things as they fully are. From that viewpoint, the issue of hell may look very different. In fact, something like that must occur. Given that heaven will be perfect without tears or grief (**Revelation 21:4**), hell will not be allowed 'to spoil the party'.

Ultimately, as with so many difficult issues, we must trust in the fact that we have a God of both justice and love and that any solution will reflect both those characteristics. *Perfectly.*

33

CAN THOSE WHO COMMIT SUICIDE GO TO HEAVEN?

Suicide is tragic, not just for those who commit it but for all the family and friends. In the UK, figures for registered deaths by suicide are between 5,000 and 6,000 a year but it's accepted that the real figure is much higher; many suicides are treated as deaths due to 'unknown causes' or 'household accidents'. That's a lot of grief for a lot of people.

Here I want to focus on this specific question: does committing suicide eliminate any possibility of a joyful eternity with Christ?

Although suicide is defined as the act of voluntarily and intentionally taking your own life, in reality not all suicide is the same. Consider the following cases of people who have chosen to take their own lives.

- A teenage girl in a culture that values honour and virginity who has been raped.

- A leader of the French Resistance, being brutally tortured by the Nazis, who realises that he is close to revealing the names of his comrades.
- A man, deeply disappointed and depressed, who finds no point in life.
- A Christian believer who is told they must take part in sacrifices to other gods.
- A woman, aware she has incurable and progressive dementia, who thinks she will be an unsupportable burden to her family.

There are others. Is a soldier throwing himself on a grenade to save his comrades suicide? Was Samson's death suicide? (See **Judges 16:28-30**.)

One helpful distinction is whether the motive was for self or for others. We also must bear in mind that we cannot know the exact state of mind of those who commit suicide. The standard phrase from coroners in such cases is worth remembering: the act was done while 'the balance of mind was disturbed'.

This question about the eternal fate of someone who commits suicide doubtless arises from the fact that the church has for centuries had a very negative attitude towards suicide. Within the first centuries of the church, suicidal actions came under increasing theological condemnation. Suicide, as 'self-murder', was a breach of the sixth commandment 'You shall not murder' (**Exodus 20:13**). It was seen, too, as an act of defiance against God, the sovereign author of existence and the only one with the authority to give and take life. A key factor in the thinking of the Catholic Church was the belief that Christians should, before death, be given the Last Rites, a ritual that included repentance and the priestly pronouncement of forgiveness. By eliminating all possibility of this, suicide was a barrier to eternal salvation. It's difficult to be sympathetic about the attitude of the church here but it is worth commenting that, given how many suicides are due to depressive episodes which may go away on their own, these prohibitions against suicide may have helped some weather the storm and come out the other side.

From the sixteenth century, attitudes to suicide changed. The church Reformers taught the biblical view that salvation is all about having a right relationship with Christ through faith. On that basis, although 'tidying matters up' at the end of your life is a good idea, a failure to do so is not something with eternal consequences. The new focus on the Bible also reminded people of the power of depression and its role in such cases of suicide. Although the six cases of suicide noted in the Bible are never viewed favourably, many key biblical characters had moments of great personal distress. Solomon reached the point where he 'hated life' (**Ecclesiastes 2:17**), Elijah was depressed and prayed to die (**1 Kings 19:4**), Jonah expressed the same sentiment (**Jonah 4:8**) and even Paul 'despaired of life itself' (**2 Corinthians 1:8**), and to these can be added the depths plumbed by such people as Job, David and Jeremiah. With this change in emphasis came a new honesty. So the great Victorian preacher C.H. Spurgeon was open with his struggle against depression and referred to it in his preaching and writing. Significantly, in 1907 the Salvation Army set up an Anti-Suicide Bureau, in many ways a precursor to the Samaritans, which had a great impact in reducing suicide numbers.

So can those who commit suicide go to heaven? Let me make some cautious comments.

- **First,** as noted at the start, suicide is not a one-size-fits-all moral event.

- **Second,** how a life is lived is far more important than how it ends. We go to heaven through becoming a child of God by faith in Christ (**John 3:16**; **Ephesians 2:8-9**; **Romans 8:31-33**) and I see no evidence that God ever rejects his adopted children.

- **Third,** despite expressing sympathy for those so tempted, suicide remains wrong and sinful. In addition to the traditional criticisms, it demonstrates a failure of the three great Christian virtues: faith, hope and love.

> Suicide displays a lack of faith that God is with you, a lack of hope that things can be better and a lack of love for those who will be hurt by the suicide. It's worth remembering that although believers are saved through grace, there is still some sort of assessment or even judgement for how they have lived (**1 Corinthians 3:10-15**).

Let me remind you that there are today enormous resources for those tempted to suicide. If so needed, we should seek them ourselves and we should certainly do our best to offer them to those struggling with any temptation to 'end it all'. We are in the business of compassion, not condemnation.

Finally, let me end by simply quoting **Psalm 34:18**, 'The LORD is close to the broken-hearted and saves those who are crushed in spirit.' *Amen.*

34

WILL I BE BALD IN HEAVEN?

Let me declare an interest. With my own hairline receding, whether hair loss is an eternal condition interests me. In the previous book I answered the question 'Will I be fat in heaven?' and while this question touches the same ground there's a lot that's different.

Baldness and hair loss, whether for men or women, is often viewed negatively. It is associated with ageing, physical decline and a loss of vitality or even virility, although it may have no link with any of them. To balance this, in some cultures baldness is seen as a sign of maturity and is linked with wisdom. Nevertheless, popular culture has had a tendency to promote 'the full head of hair', so that in the past it was deemed essential for Hollywood heroes to have a generous covering of hair, even if it had to be glued on!

Thankfully, here cultural values are changing. There are many encouragements today to accept hair loss, many now celebrate baldness and some even choose to cultivate the bald look.

So it is now perfectly normal to have films where the male lead is either naturally bald or has cultivated baldness: think of Patrick Stewart, Dwayne Johnson, Ben Kingsley and Jason Statham. In sport, too, the absence of hair is increasingly common. Nevertheless, people still feel self-conscious about baldness and it can lead to such issues as low self-esteem or 'body image dissatisfaction'.

There's little in the Bible about baldness and what's present is not easy to interpret because it may refer to a shaved head. Ritual head-shaving was something widely practised: sometimes as part of a purification or consecration ritual (**Numbers 6:5, 18; 8:7; Acts 18:18**), as an act of mourning (**Job 1:20**) or in repentance (**Micah 1:16**). One odd reference to baldness needs mentioning. In **2 Kings 2:23-24** we are told the uncomfortable tale of the prophet Elisha being mocked by some youths on account of his baldness and responding with a curse that was dramatically fulfilled by a pair of bears. What's happening here is not entirely clear but some commentators suggest that the youths may have been mocking Elisha, not so much for any natural baldness, but for the fact that his shaved head showed he was a prophet of the Lord. So I'm not sure it adds very much to any discussion of natural baldness.

So must those Christians who are 'follicly challenged' look forward to being 'hair-free for eternity'? Let me remind you that the only evidence we have about our eternal status comes from what the Bible tells us and the descriptions we have of the appearances of Jesus after his resurrection, where he acts as some kind of a prototype of what we will be in eternity. And let me give you a caution. In the letter of **1 John**, the author – the disciple John – says this: 'Dear friends, now we are children of God, and what we will be has not yet been made known. But we know that when Christ appears, we shall be like him, for we shall see him as he is' (**1 John 3:2**). Note that phrase 'what we will be has not yet been made known'. If Saint John confesses his lack of knowledge, who am I to claim it?

What we can be confident of are three things: transformation, continuation and consolation.

There will be *transformation*. The biblical teaching is that we who have put our faith in Christ will have glorified bodies. It says in **1 Corinthians 15:42-44** that, in contrast to our current perishable and frail physical bodies, our resurrected bodies will be imperishable, glorious and spiritual. We are not told what in practice that will look like. It's worth pondering on the fact that the resurrected Jesus could appear in a room with doors locked (**John 20:19**). In our present existence, matter – atoms, molecules, compounds – rules us; in eternity, will we rule matter? Here we can only speculate but, if so, then might we be able to change what we look like? Mind you, I confess to a profound unease that, as in some very bad television soap opera, we will all have glistening hair and gleaming teeth. In fact, it's worth remembering that this heavenly transformation will also extend to our attitudes. Whereas on earth there is a tendency to prize what we consider to be bodily perfection and despise physical failings, in heaven all will be different. No one will think less of us for such things as baldness and indeed we may be able to rejoice in it.

There will be *continuation*. A key point here is that in heaven, even if we are transformed, we will remain who we are. Just as the risen Jesus was recognised by his disciples and, indeed, still possessed the scars of his crucifixion, so too will we be recognisable in eternity. How we square transformation and continuation is something I look forward to finding out. All I can offer is that there are times in this life, when as you look at an elderly person, past and present come together and you can glimpse how they looked when they were young. Does something similar occur in eternity? Will we be seen at the same time as who we once were on earth and who we are in glory? I don't know and no one living does.

There will be *consolation*. In Revelation 21:4 we read the wonderfully comforting words, '"He will wipe every tear from their eyes. There will be no more death" or mourning or crying or pain, for the old order of things has passed away.' On that basis, we can confidently say that if baldness or any other physical feature is causing us unhappiness here, then it won't 'up there'. There'll be a lot better things to do than worry about our hair – or lack of it!

PART EIGHT

THE CHURCH AND LIFE

35

WHY CAN'T I FIND A LOCAL CHURCH THAT I'M COMFORTABLE WITH?

Although most Christians are happy with their local church, some struggle to find a spiritual home. So they continue drifting around churches or end up as those who describe themselves as having 'given up on the church, but not on Christ'. Skipping involvement in local church is an old problem but three factors have made it worse. The first is that access to cars has enlarged the possibilities for church hunting. The second, more recent, is that during the COVID pandemic, the discovery of online services often fuelled a discontent with a real-world church. The third is that we live in an age where a consumer mentality dominates so that the test for everything is simply 'does this please me?'

There are many reasons for discomfort with a church. It might be the preaching and what is taught (or not taught), the warmth (or otherwise) of the fellowship, the style of music and so on.

Not all discomfort with a church is wrong. It can be a way of telling you something is wrong with the church: perhaps a teaching that denies the authority of the Bible, an ungracious attitude to other Christians, unhealthy attitudes to money or perhaps a leadership that is dominating or controlling. Here, after thought and prayer, it may be right to tiptoe elsewhere. But in most cases behind the inability to find a 'comfortable' local church is a spiritual restlessness.

For such people let me offer four responses.

First, *counsel:* you may never find a church you are comfortable in. At the heart of spiritual restlessness is the fantasy – even the lie – that *somewhere* out there is a perfect church. The perfect church is the pot of gold at the end of the rainbow; always just over the horizon. Be content with a real ordinary church, not some imaginary perfect one.

Second, *a command:* you are ordered to be in a local church. The New Testament offers no support for any unending church hunt but orders us to 'do church'. **Hebrews 10:25** talks of 'not giving up meeting together, as some are in the habit of doing, but encouraging one another'. Although we tend to see salvation as something done for us as *individuals*, the Bible sees salvation as oriented around a *community*. One of the chief manifestations of sin in humanity is how we are divided against each other in disunity, hatred and conflict. God's response in Christ is to create a new people of God out of every race, language (for example **Ephesians 1:22-23; 3:10-11; Revelation 7:9-10**). In the local church we see, on a small, prototype scale, the glorious reunification of our shattered world in Christ. By turning up and being involved we are showing our solidarity and involvement with the glorious church of eternity. The local church is not something we are invited to for our pleasure but something we are commanded to be involved in as our duty.

Third, *a caution:* a comfortable local church may hinder you. Many Christians misunderstand the purpose of the local church. They see it as being like a social club, a theatre or a concert and, as such, only a little more than sanctified entertainment. Yet the New Testament's picture of the local church is very different and is far more focused on our needs than our desires. It is a place where we are taught, trained, nurtured and healed. It is where, through teaching and fellowship with one another, we can be encouraged, challenged or comforted, and our head knowledge and heart experience of the Christian faith applied, tested and adjusted. One problem with 'a church that makes me feel comfortable' is that it is like the internet phenomenon whereby people only visit those web pages or groups which hold similar views to theirs, with the result that, unchallenged, they live in an echo-chamber that endlessly reinforces their views. We need to be somewhere where our views and prejudices are not confirmed, and there is a lot to be said for being in a church where, as long as it is not on fundamental truth, you don't agree with everything. Local church is like sandpaper, wielded by a skilled carpenter, that wears away the rough edges of our lives. Yes, there are times when church is neither enjoyable nor comfortable but it's perfectly possible that that's when it is doing us most good.

Fourth, *a challenge:* be committed to your local church. New Testament believers would take a dim view of the idea that belonging to church meant no more than a presence at a service for an hour or so. A local church is our spiritual family with whom we share, care, give and pray together, and a Sunday meeting is just the most visible demonstration of this. Here, I have to say digital or online services are inadequate. They require no effort and no commitment and can be turned off whenever we choose. Yes, there are situations of health, disability, family or transport that demand we stay tuned in to something online. God wants us to be *physically* with others, to bond with them over conversation and to give – and receive – smiles, handshakes and hugs. It's worth remembering that God made a central part of Christian fellowship the very physical act of sharing bread and wine. And you can't do that online. Ironically, the more you are committed to a church, the more likely you are to be comfortable with it.

As with many other things, the more you put in, the more you get out. Get involved in your local fellowship. Commitment, more than comfort, brings contentment in church.

36

HAVE I TRULY ACCEPTED JESUS?

Two questions are often asked: have I genuinely put my faith in Jesus and can I be confident that, at death, I will enter into God's eternal kingdom? I will comment on both of these here and in the answer to Question 37. These are challenging queries. Not only do they involve eternal and spiritual matters that are hidden from us, but any careless answers risk either false confidence or needless alarm.

A reminder. To be a Christian is not simply to 'admire Jesus' or 'seek to follow his teaching'. It is to submit to him as our personal Lord and the one who died to save us. To make that submission is to undergo what the Bible calls 'being born again' (**John 3:3-7; 1 Peter 1:3, 23; Titus 3:5; 1 John 5:1**). This is a supernatural event that involves receiving forgiveness, adoption into God's family and being sealed by the Holy Spirit (**Ephesians 1:13**).

Whether we have indeed been born again is an important question. In **Matthew 7:22-23** Jesus warns, 'Many will say to me on that day, "Lord, Lord, did we not prophesy in your name and in your name drive out demons and in your name perform many miracles?" Then I will tell them plainly, "I never knew you. Away from me, you evildoers!"'

Although there is no absolute sure-fire test of a new spiritual life, there are a number of hallmarks of an authentic faith. Let me outline them.

1) *A point of conversion.* To become a Christian needs a conversion. For some, conversion is a dramatic and memorable occasion that, in mere instants, utterly transforms their life. For others, becoming a Christian is more protracted. However it occurs, and at what pace, conversion is not just a decision but something that involves confession of sin, repentance and faith in Christ.

To become a Christian is to accept Jesus as nothing less than *Lord*. If we imagine our life as a car, what we do in conversion is let Jesus take the driving seat. To say to Jesus, 'You are Lord but of only some part of my life,' is to deny him his claim to be Lord *of all*.

2) *A changed life.* Any authentic acceptance of Jesus must involve a change in how we live. There will be wrong things (words, deeds, relationships) to be rejected and good things (kindness, forgiveness, love, etc.) to be sought. Jesus said, 'By their fruit you will recognise them' (**Matthew 7:16**) and a changed life is one of the clearest evidences of genuine faith. This change in life is due to the collaboration between our choice and the power of the Holy Spirit. Ultimately, there needs to be evidence of the 'fruit of the Spirit' (**Galatians 5:22-23**): 'love, joy, peace, forbearance, kindness, goodness, faithfulness, gentleness and self-control'.

Here note that committing some sin is not *necessarily* an indication that we aren't a child of God. The case of Peter denying Jesus is a classic example. If we stumble and fall into the dirt, we should pick ourselves up, seek forgiveness and get on with the Christian life. If, however, we find we rather enjoy rolling in the dirt, then that might indicate that our faith lacks any authentic basis.

3) An awareness of the Holy Spirit. Here we are in an area of personal experience. The Bible is clear that to become a Christian is to receive the gift of the Holy Spirit (**Acts 2:38; Romans 8:9; 1 Corinthians 6:19; Galatians 4:6**). Although we may not have had any dramatic experience of the Holy Spirit we should nevertheless have had some times where we sensed him comforting, challenging or consoling us. Today many Christians simply think of the Holy Spirit in terms of the *gifts*, such as prophecy, healing or speaking in tongues. Yet in terms of confirming a genuine faith, it is the fruit of the Spirit (**Galatians 5:22-23**) that is far more important.

4) *A delight in God.* One indicator of a genuine conversion is that we desire to know more of God and take a deep interest in prayer. There is, as well, a pleasure in acquiring a more profound understanding of the Bible and, in it, hearing God speaking to us. We delight, too, in being with God's people in worship and fellowship. We may not enjoy every song, agree with every sermon or want to hug every believer, but overall, our meetings together are a joy more than a duty. A particularly helpful indicator of authentic faith here is a love for one another: 'We know that we have passed from death to life, because we love each other' (**1 John 3:14**).

5) *The public confession of Christ.* There are times, places and cultures where concealing our Christian faith is excusable and indeed necessary. Most of us, however, do not live in such situations. A good but not infallible indicator of an authentic Christian faith is that we share the good news of the gospel freely and happily (see **Romans 10:9**). The public declaration of our faith, particularly in baptism, is another important marker of authentic conversion.

6) *An enduring faith.* We live in an urgent age and we want instant diagnoses so it's frustrating that perhaps the best test for authentic Christianity is whether it stays the course. The surest proof that our acceptance of Jesus was genuine is undoubtedly how, through good and through bad, it lasts and produces fruit. 'But the one that stands firm to the end will be saved' (**Matthew 24:13**).

Let me make a final comment. It's vital that we make sure that our faith is authentic. But once we've done that, it's important to press on with living out our faith. A failure to do that makes us like those foolish gardeners who are constantly digging up the seeds they have planted to see if they are sprouting. Our task is to generate fruit, not constantly inspect our roots.

37

WHAT HAPPENS IF I CONTINUE TO SIN AFTER ACCEPTING JESUS?

As I mentioned previously, Christians commonly wrestle with two questions: am I genuinely saved and am I going to make it to heaven? Earlier in this book (Question 20) I discussed the issue of whether a Christian can lose their salvation and offered my view that if you have become a child of God through Christ, nothing can take away your salvation: 'once saved, always saved'. This raises another question: what happens if, as a Christian, we sin?

Let me remind you of some basics. We can only be saved by taking Christ's death on the cross as payment for our sins. Accepting that gracious offer results in a dramatic change: we are no longer God's enemies but his loved sons and daughters. *Wonderful!* Nevertheless, the New Testament has many passages which talk about everybody being judged by God on the basis of what they have done, resulting in both penalties and rewards. The fullest passage is **Matthew 25:31-46** – the

Parable of the Sheep and the Goats – which suggests that judgement is based on how we have treated others, especially those in need. There are others.

- **Matthew 16:27:** 'For the Son of Man is going to come in his Father's glory with his angels, and then he will reward each person according to what they have done.'
- **John 5:28-29:** 'A time is coming when all who are in their graves will hear his voice and come out – those who have done what is good will rise to live, and those who have done what is evil will rise to be condemned.'
- **2 Corinthians 5:10:** 'For we must all appear before the judgement seat of Christ, so that each of us may receive what is due to us for the things done while in the body, whether good or bad.'
- **Revelation 22:12:** 'Look, I am coming soon! My reward is with me, and I will give to each person according to what they have done.'

This question asks what happens 'if I *continue* to sin' and I think it is helpful here to distinguish between isolated sinful actions – flashes of, say, anger, pride, greed or lust – and a continuing, sustained rebellion against God. The New Testament accepts we will sin. Yes, we are washed clean by Christ but in the course of life our 'clean clothes' get stained and we must repent and seek forgiveness;

something that the Lord's Prayer highlights. To *continue* to sin, however, is a lasting and stubborn determination to do what is knowingly wrong.

Let me make three points.

First, *to continue to sin suggests that we haven't understood grace.* The Protestant Church has generally seen the matter of sin and grace as being like some formal judicial process where, having been charged with a crime, the judge declares us innocent and that is that: we walk out of the court with the matter behind us. Increasingly, though, there is a realisation that this kind of legal forgiveness is not what the Bible is referring to.

There, as in many parts of the world today including the Middle East, gifts bring obligations. To accept a gift, whether something tangible like a present or intangible like forgiveness, is to enter into a relationship with the one who gives it. It is to be bonded with the giver; to say, in a profound sense, 'I'll always be in your debt.' In English, when someone does us a favour, we often say something like 'Thanks! I owe you one' and that points to the same idea. In offering us forgiveness God says, in effect, 'I'm going to forgive you and make you my children', but with that comes the obligation to live like God's sons and daughters. For someone claiming to be a Christian to persistently disregard God's instructions suggests they haven't understood grace and that they may need to re-examine the basis of their faith.

Second, *to continue to sin is to invite unhappiness in this life*. God's laws are not just arbitrary rules but the best way to live. Christians who are continuously sinful will find they are neither able to experience the pleasures that non-believers have nor to have the joyful happiness of a strong relationship with God as Father.

Third, *to continue to sin is to expect a judgement in eternity.* In trying to harmonise the biblical teaching on forgiveness by grace with the warnings of judgement, the commonest conclusion is that although God's children will be exempt from the universal judgement of the world, they will face a separate assessment. This is referred to by Paul in **1 Corinthians 3:12-15**: 'If anyone builds on this foundation using gold, silver, costly stones, wood, hay or straw, their work will be shown for what it is, because the Day will bring it to light. It will be revealed with fire, and the fire will test the quality of each person's work. If what has been built survives, the builder will receive a reward. If it is burned up, the builder will suffer loss but yet will be saved – even though only as one escaping through the flames.' This implies that although believers are saved from hell, they will be tested and judged by God.

Although the word Jesus used for God as Father, 'Abba', is often translated as 'Daddy', a better translation is something like 'Papa' and many of us can remember very uncomfortable interactions with even the most loving of parents. Note, however, that this idea of judgement is not totally negative. Eternal rewards will be given!

Taken with the previous answer, the advice for the Christian is clear. Make sure you have accepted God's offer of forgiveness and adoption into his family. And in all you do, live out that status as a child of God. Remember, too, that at some point – possibly sooner than you think – all that you do will be evaluated by your heavenly Father, whether for rebuke or reward. May it be the latter!

38

IF I'M CONVERTED, DO I HAVE TO GIVE EVERYTHING AWAY?

Should Christians give away everything? It's an easy question to ask, but a harder one to answer. We may want an easy, simple response but here, as elsewhere, Christianity forces us to think.

Let me begin with three fundamental points.

First, *wealth is a gift of God.* God is a God of riches not poverty. On page one of the Bible we see him putting humanity not in some barren desert, but in a rich, fruit-filled garden. Wealth is good and can be used for good: it makes our existence bearable, our ambitions achievable and our generosity possible. After all, it's hard to be charitable to the poor if you don't have anything to give them. What the Bible does do is downplay the significance of wealth; God is more interested in the spiritual state of individuals than their finances. So, for instance, Abraham, Job and Solomon seem to have been very rich indeed.

Although it is evident that Jesus himself lived a life of poverty (**Matthew 8:20**) and on occasions demanded it of others (**Luke 18:18-25**), he had wealthy friends: for instance, Joseph of Arimathea (**Matthew 27:57-60**), Nicodemus (**John 3:1-21; 19:39-40**) and the women who supported him and his disciples (**Luke 8:2-3**). And although the early church was full of the poor, it also contained the rich; something seen in the tensions in Corinth (**1 Corinthians 11:17-34**) and elsewhere (**1 Timothy 6:17-19**).

Second, *wealth comes with dangers*. Nevertheless, despite the goodness of wealth, the Bible warns it is perilous territory for the health of the soul. All God's gifts can be turned into traps and wealth is definitely one of them. So in **Matthew 19:23-24** we read, 'Then Jesus said to his disciples, "Truly I tell you, it is hard for someone who is rich to enter the kingdom of heaven. Again I tell you, it is easier for a camel to go through the eye of a needle than for someone who is rich to enter the kingdom of God."'

Here let me point out the following dangers.

- Wealth *deceives* us that it is God. Human beings can easily turn what is good into being God and so can seek the gifts and not the giver. Wealth promises status, achievement, comfort and security but these are all things that in a richer, more permanent way, God offers to us in Christ. Wealth sets itself up as a replacement for God so that the money and the possessions it brings can become treacherous idols. The desire for wealth and 'things' becomes greed and as Jesus warns, 'Watch out! Be on your guard against all kinds of greed; life does not consist in an abundance of possessions' (**Luke 12:15**).

- Wealth can *divert* us from living for God. Wealth has an unnerving habit of slipping through the fingers and so requires constant watchfulness. 'Things', in particular, can become extraordinarily demanding, necessitating constant protection, maintenance and upkeep. We imagine our possessions to be our servants but in reality they become our masters. In the Parable of the Sower Jesus talks of seed that 'fell among thorns, which grew up and choked the plants, so that they did not bear grain' (**Mark 4:7**). In **Mark 4:18-19** he explains this as how 'the worries of this life, the deceitfulness of wealth and the desires for other things come in and choke the word, making it unfruitful'. Things easily strangle us into spiritual apathy. At its worst, the pursuit of wealth can lead us into many errors: 'For the love of money is a root of all kinds of evil' (**1 Timothy 6:10**).

- Wealth *denies* us contentment from God. The answer to the question, 'How much more do I need?' is always, 'Just a little bit more.' To seek fulfilment through things is like trying to catch your own shadow: it can't be done. Riches never last and ultimately even the richest person is robbed of every possession they have by death.

Hebrews 13:5 offers a corrective view: 'Keep your lives free from the love of money and be content with what you have, because God has said, "Never will I leave you; never will I forsake you."'

Third, *wealth demands the right response.* The risks of wealth mean we need an intelligent, prayerful response. Let me offer some brief guidelines.

- ***Wealth requires a personal solution.*** I have no idea why God gives some people riches and others poverty. What is important is that we are made by God as individuals. Some people may be untroubled by the temptations of wealth while others may find that their weakness lies in this area. One size doesn't fit all and we should be wary of judging 'someone else's servant' (Romans 14:4).

- ***Wealth is loaned, not owned.*** We talk about our own finances as our money. However, nothing of what we have is, strictly speaking, ours. It all comes from God, is owned by God, and ultimately how we have used or abused it will be reviewed by God.

- ***Wealth is the opportunity for blessing.*** There should be a voluntary principle in churches that 'those who have, help those who haven't'. It was a practice of the early church (Acts 2:44-45; 4:32-35) and, if wisely implemented, has validity.

- ***Wealth needs limits.*** Even if Jesus does not want us to take on a life of poverty, he wants us to live responsibly. These days we have become aware that the pursuit of things doesn't just cost us, but also God's creation. There are various ways of interpreting the idea of an environmental footprint. But it's a good idea to tread lightly on what God has made.

Ultimately all Christians face a choice between either serving wealth or God's kingdom. In **Matthew 6:24** we read, 'You cannot serve both God and Money.' Does a Christian have to give everything away? Not necessarily, but I think we need to be prepared to do so if God tells us.

39

WHY CAN THE CHRISTIAN LIFE BE A STRUGGLE?

Although most Christians are happy in their faith there are those who can find things difficult. What particularly puzzles many Christians is that, having come over to God's side, they find their life has become harder rather than easier. Let me offer some thoughts.

First, struggles are *unavoidable for the Christian*. One reason many Christians have struggles is that they have come to believe their lives should permanently overflow with peace, joy and victory. This view fits with our culture which majors on feeling good and prefers to ignore difficulties. The reality is that while there are many tremendous joys and encouragements in being a Christian, to commit yourself to Christ – and to mean it – is to sign up for struggle and conflict in this life.

One reason is that our world, fallen from God, is not neutral. It is like a permanently active down-escalator so that morally, life always tends towards what is wrong. As a result, to stand for God's values is like swimming against the flow or cycling uphill. The opposition the world offers is heightened by two things. One is that our own desires are corrupted so that such things as pride, greed and lust are deeply rooted in our minds (**Galatians 5:19-21**). Another is that we are opposed by the supernatural powers of evil that seek to defeat God's people (**1 Peter 5:8**).

In becoming a Christian we have put ourselves on a battlefield, and that we must face hostility is repeatedly taught in the New Testament. Jesus himself warned that those who followed him would be reviled and persecuted (**Matthew 5:10-12; John 15:18-20**) and Paul gave a similar warning (**Acts 14:21-22; Romans 8:35-36; 2 Timothy 3:12**). **Philippians 1:29** expresses this conflict: 'For it has been granted to you on behalf of Christ not only to believe in him, but also to suffer for him.'

Note that to surrender in this spiritual conflict is not only wrong, it is also ineffectual. Those who have given up on the spiritual battle do not find peace, only discouragement and despair. Sadly, too, there are always new depths that the defeated can be dragged down to. We must fight!

Second, struggles are *considerable for the Christian*. There's much traditional wisdom, sadly overlooked today, about spiritual battles. The warfare waged against us is subtle, varied and persistent.

- It is *subtle*. There are direct attacks in which we are openly tempted by such things as anger, greed, lust or lying. But there are also attacks by stealth. So, for instance, we may find ourselves in some work or social environment where our commitment to honesty is steadily and imperceptibly undermined. Equally, we may feel we have achieved a victory over some particular temptation only to fall into some sinful sense of pride and superiority about it.

- It is *varied*. So, for instance, having identified that anger is a weakness, we may resolve not to get angry in a difficult situation. But in doing so our focus on anger may have left us open to other sins.

- It is *persistent*. We may find that we've successfully managed to resist some particular temptation for weeks. But the attack may continue, perhaps for months or years.

None of the great saints of God ever treated temptation lightly and neither should we.

Third, struggles are *bearable for the Christian*. All this may sound discouraging but let me give you five brief encouragements.

1) Spiritual struggles are a sign of life. It's all too easy to imagine that we face opposition because we have failed. That's what the diabolic powers would like us to feel. In reality, being tempted may indicate that we are spiritually alive and making progress. After all, the devil doesn't waste his energies on the spiritually dead. Ironically, the time to get worried in your Christian life is not when things are going badly, but when, in every area, you are met with success.

2) Struggles are essential for our maturing as Christians. We all recognise the value of pain and effort in such things as physiotherapy or sports training. The same principle applies to our spiritual life: we need opposition to grow. Doctors have noted that extended stays in the zero gravity of the International Space Station are deeply harmful for the body. Physically, the human body needs gravity to work against; similarly, spiritual zero gravity is harmful to our life with God. We need to exercise muscles of faith and for that we need forces opposing us.

3) Struggles keep us close to God. The howl of a wolf will make sheep press closer to the shepherd. One of the great secrets of the Christian life is that, paradoxically, when we are weak we are strong because we are forced to rely on Christ. As **2 Corinthians 12:9** says, God's 'power is made perfect in weakness'. When we feel weak or inadequate we are forced to lean on God and trust him to carry us through.

4) We do not fight struggles on our own. Our diabolic opposition likes us to imagine we are fighting on our own. The reality is otherwise. As believers in Christ we have been given the Holy Spirit to help us, his armour (**Ephesians 6**) and have access to our loving heavenly Father through prayer. There is also the wisdom granted us through the Bible and support of other believers in our churches.

5) Our struggles have limits. Finally, our loving and merciful God has set limits on how long and how strong our struggle will be (**1 Corinthians 10:13**). We also need to remember that sooner or later either we go to Christ or he will come to us.

In 2 Corinthians 4:17 Paul writes, 'For our light and momentary troubles are achieving for us an eternal glory that far outweighs them all.' Ultimately, the issue about spiritual struggles is not the question 'why?' but our need to continue to fight in them. *Be encouraged!*

THE LAST WORD

40

IS IT JUST CHRISTIANS WHO FACE TRICKY QUESTIONS?

In these thirty-nine answers I've done my best to clarify many particular elements of Christian belief. I'm well aware that some of you reading this will not (yet) be Christians and it has crossed my mind that some may ask whether, with so many tricky questions, the Christian faith can be credible. Not only do I believe it is credible but I would point out that other positions of faith – and we all believe in something – face questions too. So here I thought I would use the opportunity to turn the tables. I can't address every form of belief so let me direct myself to those who, whether atheists, agnostics or 'uncertain', would still be sceptical of the Christian faith. I should also apologise that this answer is far longer than the others.

Let me first ask some foundational questions.

Do you have a sound basis for your scepticism?

Many people would mutter something about their faith in 'science' as defence against the very possibility of God, the supernatural and miracles. Here my scientist friends remind me that such confidence is not as solidly based as it once seemed. At every level, everything seems much more complicated than once assumed. We now know that atoms are not solid little ball bearings but complex miniature solar systems, largely full of empty space in which subatomic particles exist, most of which are themselves made up of further space and further particles. Another challenge: what exactly is 'time'? We measure it and treat it as a dimension but is it real or is it an illusion? What is it made of? And is space nothing or something we just can't detect? Oh, and let's not ignore quantum physics or mechanics where words such as 'incomprehensible', 'paradoxical' and 'contradictory' are part of normal vocabulary. For all our knowledge, the universe remains as complex and unknown as ever and probably more so. Ultimately, scepticism about God remains an act of faith.

On what basis are you certain that reality exists?

Here we enter very troubling matters. Can you prove that you and the world existing around you are real rather than apparent? Might it not be a dream? Perhaps some extraordinary *Matrix*-type simulation generated by a computer of awesome power? A number of people, some highly-educated, believe this to be credible. Although imagining that everything is illusory is probably dangerous for your mental health, it's impossible to prove that 'reality' is real. We may believe we live in a real, solid world but that belief is another act of faith.

Can you trust your own reasoning?

Arguments by sceptics frequently use words like 'logic', 'reason' and 'proof', and assume that our brain processes are reliable and can be trusted. Yet if ultimately our brains are simply the end product of purposeless, random processes operating over time, why should we trust them and their conclusions? It's another act of faith.

Can you rule out the supernatural?

The only Christianity I'm interested in is the traditional supernatural form of the faith. Scepticism rejects this, holding that we and our universe exist in a 'closed box' in which no force or fact can enter from 'beyond'. It is a balloon of philosophical faith that would be popped by even a single miracle, however tiny. Yet the problem is that across many cultures there are numerous records of events that are claimed as supernatural. And while many may be dismissed as coincidences, delusions or hallucinations, a residue remain that cannot be explained away. And once you admit that, to borrow Hamlet's words, 'there are more things in Heaven and Earth, than are dreamt of in your philosophy', you have thrown the door wide open to the possibility of God. Indeed the way that even in allegedly sceptical societies, beliefs such as tarot, astrology, crystal healing and spiritualism are widespread, and that popular culture delights in magic and the supernatural is suggestive. It seems that not only does the supernatural exist, but we seem to be hard-wired for it.

Let's move on to specifics.

Why is everything in the universe just right for life?

Scientists point out that one of the most extraordinary features of the universe is what they call 'fine tuning'; the way that a large number of constants (between 20 or 30) in physics have *precisely* the values that allow a stable universe that is suitable for life and intelligence to exist. Even some atheists have conceded that the universe 'appears' to be designed. Perhaps it is!

Why does complex life on earth exist?

Modern science is reasonably confident that in some form or other life has existed on this planet for four billion years. Life is confined to the habitable zone, the biosphere, which is at most 30 kilometres thick and which, given the size of the earth, is equivalent to no more than the thickness of a sheet of paper on top of a basketball. Yet, astonishingly, in an utterly hostile universe this shallow zone where life can exist has persisted unbroken for all this time. There seems to be only two options: either the earth has been 'lucky' – on the scale of an individual repeatedly winning a national lottery – or someone, somewhere, is caring for it.

Now to human beings.

Why is there such an enormous gulf in mental ability between even the highest apes and human beings?

Yes, there are inescapable physical and anatomical similarities between us and gorillas and chimpanzees but in intellectual abilities we are worlds apart. Humans use complex language, handle abstract ideas and have vast abilities for maths, music and art. We can ponder such issues as life, death, morality, the past and the future and even our purpose. We exist in large, complex societies and can create civilisations and cultures. How has this awesome jump happened? Isn't the biblical idea of us being 'made in God's image' something seriously worth considering?

Why is there a universal sense that, for all our powers, we human beings are flawed?

Across time, geography and culture, we find people lamenting that they fall short of what they could or should be. All human beings seem to have some sense of similar moral values, use them to judge others and seek to live them out for themselves. Yet, at the same time, there is the recognition that whatever standards we hold to, we fail to live up to them. Why is there such a gap between what we want to be and what, in reality, we are? Why are we simultaneously intellectual giants and moral failures? Isn't the best explanation the Christian view that, although we are made in God's image, we have rebelled against him?

Why are we so troubled by pain, illness and death?

It's a universal feature of life that we agonise and grieve over pain, illness and death. Indeed the existence of suffering is one of the biggest objections to the Christian view of a loving God. Yet, if you are a sceptic, please note that the fact that we struggle over pain and suffering and find them tragic and 'unnatural' is very curious indeed. After all, if we have originated by some totally senseless process of evolution, then death and suffering are in fact *perfectly* natural; they are merely the cutting edge of the mechanism of natural selection that has been operating on life for billions of years. But why then haven't we got used to it? When a dog or even an infant is killed on a road because they misjudged the speed of some oncoming car, no one in their right mind says with a cold shrug, 'Well, that's just natural selection for you.' Isn't the best explanation of the grief and anger with which we all view suffering the fact that it was not part of God's good intention for this world? Do we treat suffering as unnatural because, in a deep sense, that's exactly what it is.

If we reject God where do we find any absolute moral values?

Every human being sets standards and finds themselves saying that some actions are good and some are wrong. But on what basis? Evolution alone betrays us here. If life is about no more than transmitting your DNA then let's celebrate the brutal twelfth- to thirteenth-century warlord Genghis Khan, whose genetic legacy is such that surveys in Asia suggest that today some 15 million men carry segments of his genes. Whatever evolution does, it doesn't bring morality. Although they may often be more a matter of aspiration than achievement, to treat the Bible's ethical standards as God-given seems the only firm base for moral standards.

Without God, why should we keep 'inconvenient' virtues?

There are many moral values which frankly are rather inconvenient, awkward and difficult to keep. What about forgiveness, which is so very uncomfortable to offer? What about truth? It may be vital in engineering, medicine and science but in many other areas of life, such as politics, it is a nuisance. What about charity? Why should we give to the poor at our expense? What about sacrificially caring for others? I could go on. Isn't a better hypothesis that these are part of our God-given make-up and indeed part of God's own character?

Why do people matter?

From the sceptical, secular point of view it's hard to see why individual human beings have any special value. If men and women are no more than products of random evolutionary processes then, when they are a burden to society, why shouldn't they be considered as disposable? Despite the fact that history gives examples of attempts to eradicate races and, in our age, the elimination of the 'pre-born', the elderly and the infirm is either contemplated or practised, most human beings are very uneasy with such practices. That inhibition about mistreating the weak and defenceless fits well with the idea that human beings have value by virtue of being in God's image.

In the absence of God what gives life ultimate meaning or purpose? In short, what's the point?

If we live in a universe with no meaning and no ultimate future with no afterlife or judgement by God, why bother with anything other than making ourselves as comfortable as we can for as long as we can? Such a depressing view does not, however, seem to square with the fact that we all dream dreams and very few of us anchor our lives on a foundation of futility. Having a relationship with God through Christ has revolutionary implications for the meaning of how we live.

Still with me? Let's focus in on Christianity.

What explanation do you have for the Bible?

Written across two continents in several languages over at least 1,200 years, the Bible nevertheless tells a consistent story of an almighty God reaching out in grace to flawed and failing human beings. Although there are different perspectives within its pages, there is a common theme, a set of parallels between the very beginning and the very end, and a clear central point: the life and death of one individual, Jesus of Nazareth. It's a book that claims to be written by God and shows every evidence that this is in fact the case.

What are you going to do with Jesus?

Jesus cannot be ignored and demands some sort of an explanation. The Christian view is that he was God's unique intervention of himself into human history. It's easy to deny this but if Jesus wasn't that, then who was he? We can't dismiss him as a 'legendary' figure: the historical evidence is too good and the accounts of his life are consistent with their time and culture. Furthermore, *somebody* gave the world the most elevated morality it's ever had: no committee wrote the Sermon on the Mount. There is a multiple uniqueness to Jesus that demands an explanation. Jesus offered unique teaching, claimed unique authority over humanity and nature, performed unique miracles and made unique claims to be God himself. His well-attested resurrection is also unique, as is his worship immediately after as God by his followers. Who was he if he wasn't indeed who he claimed to be?

What are you going to do about Christian values?

What is taught in the New Testament is widely agreed to be the summit of human ethics. Here we see an unparalleled marriage of a severe morality with a gracious forgiveness: law and love meet. The severe standards of the gospels judge us but the action of God, taking our punishment on himself, offers to redeem us. As historian Tom Holland points out in his book *Dominion, How the Christian Revolution Remade the World,* if we try to judge Christianity, we end up judging it by its own moral standards.

Finally, why is Christianity a success?

On a personal level, multitudes of people of every culture and time can talk about how their lives have been changed and transformed by finding Jesus Christ. A telling fact is that the transformation brought by Christ also operates at the level of nations and cultures. The countries that have the least corruption, the most rights for individuals, the strongest commitment to equality and the maximum liberty for speech, with barely an exception, you will find that they are nations that have been shaped by Christianity and the Bible. You might want to ask yourself a harsh question: why is it that those countries that people want to flee to and reside in are those whose foundations are built on a biblical Christianity? There's an uncomfortable irony in the fact that many who adopt radical or progressive beliefs or lifestyles feel most free to hold them in 'Christian' countries. Of course, Christianity has no unblemished record. There has been hypocrisy and greed, and, publicly, the faith has frequently been hijacked by nationalism and tribalism. Yet if you are considering the claims of Christianity, do bear in mind that one single, striking fact: it works.

This book is all about questions people asked me and, here, asked by me. Yet the most important question is one you must ask yourself. Which view makes the most sense of the world we live in with its paradoxical coexistence of beauty, complexity and good, and its ugliness, failures and evils? A world governed by chance and chaos that ultimately is without any hope? Or a world created by a good God and redeemed by him in Jesus Christ? That's the ultimate question.

I invite you to meet Jesus Christ, who I believe and know is 'the way, the truth and the life'.